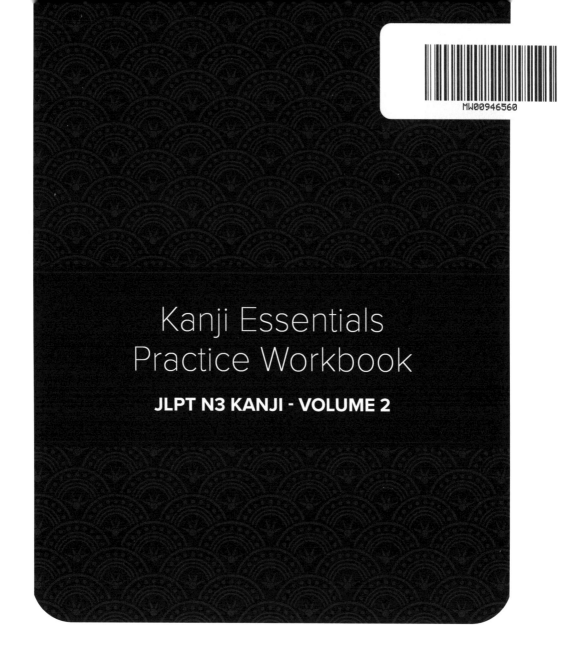

Kanji Essentials
Practice Workbook

JLPT N3 KANJI - VOLUME 2

Simon Kissinger

COPYRIGHT AND ACKNOWLEDGEMENTS

For Kanji and vocabulary definitions, this publication has included material from the JMdict (EDICT, etc.) dictionary files in accordance with the license provisions of the Electronic Dictionaries Research Group. Some entries have been altered for brevity. See http://www.edrdg.org/

Kanji stroke order diagrams in this publication are taken from the Kanji Stroke Order font by Timothy Eyre. For license and usage, see https://www.nihilist.org.uk/

DEDICATION

This book is for those who want to try different ways of learning the Japanese language. For those who love Japanese culture, history, literature, anime and JPOP fans. For those who are striving to better their Japanese language skills, aiming to pass the JLPTs. For those who plan on moving to Japan and preparing ways to cope better by learning the language beforehand. I hope this book helps you achieve success in your Japanese language learning journey.

Most of all, this book has been created with the author taking great inspiration from Hugo and Charisse- two special people who have been instrumental in making this book into reality. This book is dedicated especially to you two.

CONTENTS

PREFACE

While there is a healthy amount of learning material available out there to learn the Japanese language, there is also a healthy debate on the better methods to learn it. It is the author's intention to give students of the language effective supplemental material to help them get better at retaining what they actually learn. Japanese is beautiful in its simplicity, even poetic, deeply rich in history, and it is a language where a nation's culture can already be vividly experienced just by learning it. However, for many, it may also be quite difficult to get a hold of. This book aims to focus on the things that will help people to learn and remember information using the simplest method and when completed will serve as a solid reference book for the learner.

KANJI FEATURED IN THIS WORKBOOK

式 引 当 形 役 彼 徒 得 御 必 忘 忙 念 怒 怖 性 恐
恥 息 悲 情 想 愛 感 慣 成 戦 戻 所 才 打 払 投 折
抜 抱 押 招 指 捕 掛 探 支 放 政 敗 散 数 断 易 昔
昨 晩 景 晴 暗 暮 曲 更 最 望 期 未 末 束 杯 果 格
構 様 権 横 機 欠 次 欲 歯 歳 残 段 殺 民 求 決 治
法 泳 洗 活 流 浮 消 深 済 渡 港 満 演 点 然 煙 熱
犯 状 猫 王 現 球 産 由 申 留 番 疑 疲 痛 登 皆 盗
直 相 眠

KANJI ESSENTIALS PRACTICE WORKBOOK: JLPT N3
KANJI INTERMEDIATE I SERIES

This workbook series is the first of two series: Intermediate I and Intermediate II. The latter will focus on JLPT N2 Kanji.

HOW TO MAKE THE MOST OUT OF THIS WORKBOOK

Learning Kanji can be a daunting task to some as it requires a lot of memorization and there are over 2000 characters to learn. You must remember the shapes, the stroke order, the meaning and how to read out a character, which can be different readings depending on what word it's in. Even with some saying otherwise, there really is no getting around learning Kanji. It needs time, effort and repetition. To say it more clearly, you need to write things down.

Kanji Essentials Practice Workbook: JLPT N3 Intermediate I is a 3-book-series. As there are close to 400 characters on the N3 Kanji list, we will be breaking it down into 3 volumes. The first volume will focus only on the first list of N3 characters, while the second volume will focus on the second list of N3 Kanji as well as feature characters on the first volume. The third volume will focus on the third list of N3 characters as well as feature N3 characters from the first and second volume.

This workbook assumes that you are already up to speed with some basic Japanese vocabulary, sentence structure and some nuance in the language which you've picked up while learning the basics. Most of all, this book assumes you are comfortable enough in reading and writing both Hiragana and Katakana as these are very important first steps before learning Kanji to study Japanese.

To make the most out of this book, you need to go through each page filling all entries with the intention of completing the entire book. In the end, you'll be surprised at how much you've learned and how much information you've retained simply because you wrote things down. Furthermore, this book, when completed, will now become your own personal index for Kanji, where entries have been filled by none other than yourself.

1. Use a pencil first. Use a pen when all are final.
2. Read the Kanji Index Section first and memorize. Depending on your personal capacity, go through

SAMPLE REFERENCE SHEET

SAMPLE PRACTICE SHEET

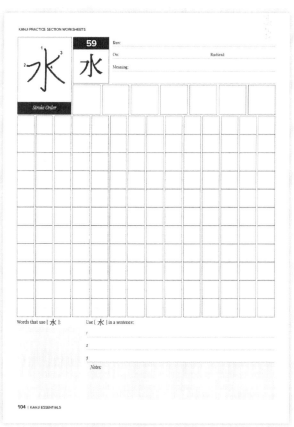

a few a day. Then once you have a firm hold of the information from the index, go directly to the practice pages and write down the information you have memorized. All Kanji in the index and practice sections can be cross-referenced via the number next to it. Now add more information in the practice pages with your own research. Add more vocabulary and use them in sentences, then note down nuances you've learned and other details like the radicals.

3. Once you have completed filling up all the pages in the practice section, move on to the reading comprehension section. Take note of the additional vocabulary and then try to translate the paragraphs in Japanese using everything you've learned so far.

私の父と母はとても仲が良く、毎週金曜日は二人で外食に出かけます。

高校生の私と小学生の弟は、となり町に住む祖父母宅へと遊びに行きます。

いつも優しく出迎えてくれる祖父母と可愛い弟と四人で一緒に過ごす金曜の夜が

私の毎週の楽しみだ。

土日に祖父母を訪れると、祖父は私たち姉弟を山や川に連れて行き色々な遊びを教えてくれる。

祖母の作る食事はとても美味しく、私たち姉弟はそれが大好きだ。

来年から私は県外の大学へと進学が決まり、毎週祖父母に会えなくなると思うととても淋しいが、

大学の長期休みには必ず会いに帰って来ると決めた。

TRANSLATION

WORDS			FURIGANA	MEANING	NOTES
景				three famous beauty spots	
				afternoon; p.m.	
				weather	
徒				pupil; student	
曜				Thursday	
週				last week; the week before	
習				study; learning; tutorial	
課				extracurricular	
曜				Tuesday	
閣	寺			Temple of the Golden Pavilion	
		止		cancelled because of rain	
週				next week	
く				to hear; to listen; to ask	
				teacher; instructor; master	
				train	
部				northern part; the north (of a region)	
あ	る			one day; (on) a certain day	
つ				one	

Your initial translation need not be perfect. Now as you do your corrections while cross-referencing the Kanji and vocabulary, you will learn things like nuance, different Kanji readings and how they are used with words. Note everything down. Translate the same Japanese paragraph again, this time taking all the new things you've understood, then you can check its English translation provided at the end of the book. If you find out there are some other things in the translation that reveals more about the words and how it was used, note them all down and revise your translation. Remember that you are now working on a N3 Kanji list, this is also a good opportunity to write down N5 and N4 Kanji you may catch as you go through this book to help you retain every Kanji you've learned up to this point.

4. This book has specially alloted spaces for writing things down so the more things you note down, the more you can take advantage of its features. Japanese has many phrases and words that does not have a direct English translation, so try to also learn by context aside from memorization when learning vocabulary and when working on the reading exercises provided in this book.

5. Schedule your time for learning. While there may possibly be some who can finish this entire book in one day, try to find the right pace that works best for you. You can try to learn and practice three to five Kanji a day or even just one, but be consistent and do the exercises regularly.

WISHING YOU THE BEST ON YOUR JAPANESE LANGUAGE LEARNING JOURNEY AND I HOPE YOU HAVE FUN WHILE YOU'RE AT IT!

がんばりましょう!

WRITING KANJI AND STROKE ORDER

Order is very important. Firstly, every stroke has a beginning, an end, and a direction. Generally, horizontal strokes travel left to right; vertical, diagonal and any bent strokes move from top to bottom, but there are exceptions.

Secondly, when you assemble strokes to make a Kanji, the process also has a beginning, an end and in compound Kanji, a direction. What comes first and what comes last? We can take a look at ten conventions which you can stick to here. If you follow these, you'll produce well-formed Kanji. In textbook illustrations, they can be numbered. Please note that the number is written at the beginning of the stroke, which tells you where to start.

THE BASICS

Before going over general rules, remember these basic strokes and order rules:

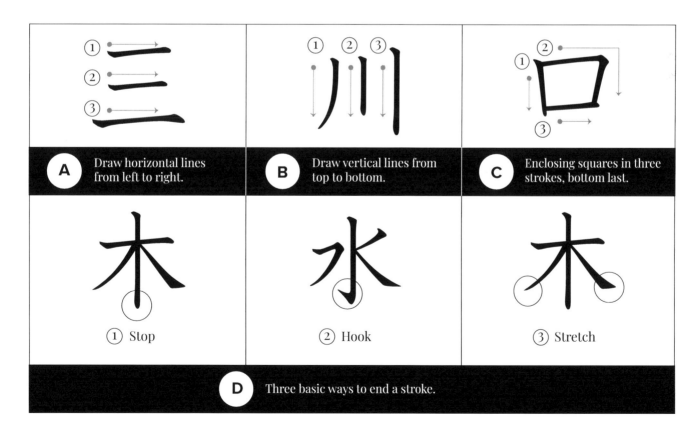

A Draw horizontal lines from left to right.

B Draw vertical lines from top to bottom.

C Enclosing squares in three strokes, bottom last.

① Stop

② Hook

③ Stretch

D Three basic ways to end a stroke.

STROKE ORDER CONVENTIONS

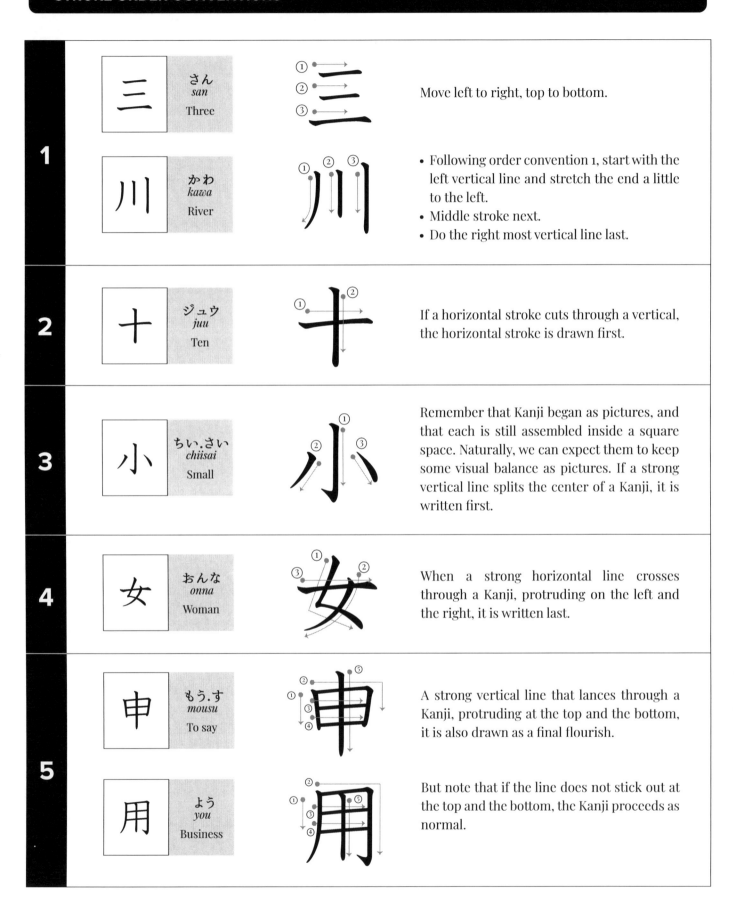

1

三 — さん / *san* — Three

Move left to right, top to bottom.

川 — かわ / *kawa* — River

- Following order convention 1, start with the left vertical line and stretch the end a little to the left.
- Middle stroke next.
- Do the right most vertical line last.

2

十 — ジュウ / *juu* — Ten

If a horizontal stroke cuts through a vertical, the horizontal stroke is drawn first.

3

小 — ちぃ.さい / *chiisai* — Small

Remember that Kanji began as pictures, and that each is still assembled inside a square space. Naturally, we can expect them to keep some visual balance as pictures. If a strong vertical line splits the center of a Kanji, it is written first.

4

女 — おんな / *onna* — Woman

When a strong horizontal line crosses through a Kanji, protruding on the left and the right, it is written last.

5

申 — もう.す / *mousu* — To say

A strong vertical line that lances through a Kanji, protruding at the top and the bottom, it is also drawn as a final flourish.

用 — よう / *you* — Business

But note that if the line does not stick out at the top and the bottom, the Kanji proceeds as normal.

6

文 | ふみ *fumi* / Sentence

When diagonal lines cross, the left-pointing line comes before the right pointing line.

7

友 | とも *tomo* / Friend

If a left-slanting line crosses a horizontal, the shorter line comes first.

Many Kanji can be thought of as enclosed by lines along the outside of the square. There are three kinds of enclosure:

A. From the top
The enclosing lines are drawn first

8

回 | まわ.る *mawaru* / To turn

B. Surrounding
The three upper sides are written first, and the bottom horizontal written last

遠 | とお.い *tooi* / Distant

C. From the bottom
We can identify the "number 3" enclosure because of its resemblance to the number, with a bottom line stretching up to the right bottom end of the inner Kanji. Whenever you see this enclosure, you must begin with the inner Kanji first.

9

犬 | いぬ *inu* / Dog

Some Kanji have a very short stroke, usually on the upper right side (犬 , 成) or occasionally the lower right side (玉 , 国). This is added to a Kanji as the last stroke.

Kanji Index
JLPT N3 - Volume 2

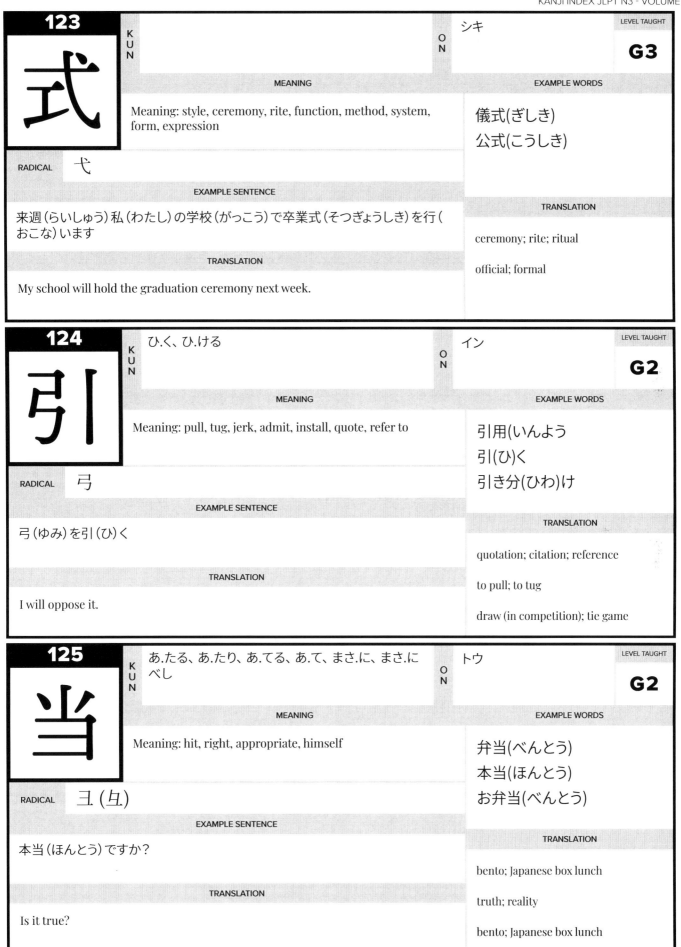

123 式

KUN

ON シキ

LEVEL TAUGHT G3

MEANING

Meaning: style, ceremony, rite, function, method, system, form, expression

RADICAL 弋

EXAMPLE SENTENCE

来週（らいしゅう）私（わたし）の学校（がっこう）で卒業式（そつぎょうしき）を行（おこな）います

TRANSLATION

My school will hold the graduation ceremony next week.

EXAMPLE WORDS

儀式（ぎしき）
公式（こうしき）

TRANSLATION

ceremony; rite; ritual

official; formal

124 引

KUN ひ.く、ひ.ける

ON イン

LEVEL TAUGHT G2

MEANING

Meaning: pull, tug, jerk, admit, install, quote, refer to

RADICAL 弓

EXAMPLE SENTENCE

弓（ゆみ）を引（ひ）く

TRANSLATION

I will oppose it.

EXAMPLE WORDS

引用（いんよう
引（ひ）く
引き分（ひわ）け

TRANSLATION

quotation; citation; reference

to pull; to tug

draw (in competition); tie game

125 当

KUN あ.たる、あ.たり、あ.てる、あ.て、まさ.に、まさ.にべし

ON トウ

LEVEL TAUGHT G2

MEANING

Meaning: hit, right, appropriate, himself

RADICAL ヨ（彑）

EXAMPLE SENTENCE

本当（ほんとう）ですか？

TRANSLATION

Is it true?

EXAMPLE WORDS

弁当（べんとう）
本当（ほんとう）
お弁当（べんとう）

TRANSLATION

bento; Japanese box lunch

truth; reality

bento; Japanese box lunch

126 形

KUN かた、-がた、かたち、なり

ON ケイ、ギョウ

LEVEL TAUGHT G2

RADICAL 彡

MEANING
Meaning: shape, form, style

EXAMPLE WORDS
人形（にんぎょう）
正方形（せいほうけい）
形容詞（けいようし）

TRANSLATION
doll; puppet; figure

square

adjective; i-adjective (in Japanese)

EXAMPLE SENTENCE
娘（むすめ）に人形（にんぎょう）をあげます

TRANSLATION
I will give my daughter a doll.

---

127 役

KUN

ON ヤク、エキ

LEVEL TAUGHT G3

RADICAL 彳

MEANING
Meaning: duty, war, campaign, drafted labor, office, service, role

EXAMPLE WORDS
役割（やくわり）
役所（やくしょ）
役（やく）に立（た）つ

TRANSLATION
part; assigning (allotment of) parts

government office; public office

to be helpful; to be useful

EXAMPLE SENTENCE
この辞書（じしょ）は役に立つ（やくにたつ）です

TRANSLATION
This dictionary is quite useful.

---

128 彼

KUN かれ、かの、か.の

ON ヒ

LEVEL TAUGHT Junior High

RADICAL 彳

MEANING
Meaning: he, that, the

EXAMPLE WORDS
彼処（あそこ）
彼（かれ）
彼女（かのじょ）

TRANSLATION
over there; that place

he; him

she; her

EXAMPLE SENTENCE
彼氏（かれし）がいますか

TRANSLATION
Do you have boyfriend?

129 徒

KUN	いたずら、あだ	ON	ト	LEVEL TAUGHT
				G4

MEANING

Meaning: on foot, junior, emptiness, vanity, futility, uselessness, ephemeral thing, gang, set, party, people

RADICAL 彳

EXAMPLE SENTENCE

こちらの学校（がっこう）は６００生徒（せいと）がいます

TRANSLATION

This school has 600 students.

EXAMPLE WORDS

生徒(せいと)
徒歩(とほ)
徒弟 (とてい)

TRANSLATION

pupil; student; schoolchild

walking; going on foot

apprentice

130 得

KUN	え.る、う.る	ON	トク	LEVEL TAUGHT
				G5

MEANING

Meaning: gain, get, find, earn, acquire, can, may, able to, profit, advantage, benefit

RADICAL 彳

EXAMPLE SENTENCE

仕事（しごと）に一番（いちばん）得意（とくい）なスキルは何（なん）ですか？

TRANSLATION

What is your best skill in this job?

EXAMPLE WORDS

説得(せっとく)
得点(とくてん)
得意(とくい)

TRANSLATION

persuasion

scoring; score

triumph; prosperity

131 御

KUN	おん-、お-、み-	ON	ギョ、ゴ	LEVEL TAUGHT
				Junior High

MEANING

Meaning: honorable, manipulate, govern

RADICAL 彳

EXAMPLE SENTENCE

御酒（おさけ）を飲（の）めますか

TRANSLATION

Can you drink wine?

EXAMPLE WORDS

御(お)
御金(おかね)
御酒(おさけ)

TRANSLATION

honorific/polite/humble prefix

money

alcohol; sake

132 必

KUN かなら.ず

ON ヒツ

LEVEL TAUGHT G4

MEANING
Meaning: invariably, certain, inevitable

RADICAL 心 (忄 , 灬)

EXAMPLE WORDS
必要(ひつよう)
必(かなら)ず
必(かなら)ずしも

EXAMPLE SENTENCE
来(こ)ない場合(ばあい)は必(かなら)ず連絡(れんらく)ください

TRANSLATION
In case you don't come, please make sure to contact me.

TRANSLATION
necessary; needed; essential

always; without exception

(not) always; (not) necessarily

133 忘

KUN わす.れる

ON ボウ

LEVEL TAUGHT G6

MEANING
Meaning: forget

RADICAL 心 (忄 , 灬)

EXAMPLE WORDS
忘(わす)れる
忘(わす)れ物(もの)
忘年会(ぼうねんかい)

EXAMPLE SENTENCE
電車(でんしゃ)の中(なか)に忘れ物(わすれもの)がありますけど

TRANSLATION
Excuse me, I left something of mine on the train.

TRANSLATION
to forget; to leave carelessly; to be forgetful of

lost article; something forgotten

year-end party; "forget-the-year" party

134 忙

KUN いそが.しい、せわ.しい、おそ.れる、うれえるさま

ON ボウ、モウ

LEVEL TAUGHT Junior High

MEANING
Meaning: busy, occupied, restless

RADICAL 心 (忄 , 灬)

EXAMPLE WORDS
忙(いそが)しい
多忙(たぼう)
忙殺(ぼうさつ)

EXAMPLE SENTENCE
今(いま)、忙(いそが)しいですか?

TRANSLATION
Are you busy right now?

TRANSLATION
busy; occupied; hectic

being very busy; busyness

being extremely busy; being swamped with work

135 念

KUN

ON ネン

LEVEL TAUGHT G4

RADICAL 心 (忄, 小)

MEANING

Meaning: wish, sense, idea, thought, feeling, desire, attention

EXAMPLE WORDS

残念(ざんねん)

記念日(きねんび)

念書(ねんしょ)

EXAMPLE SENTENCE

友達(ともだち)の結婚式(けっこんしき)を参加(さんか)できませんでした。とても残念(ざんねん)なことです

TRANSLATION

It's very unfortunate that I wasn't able to participate in my friend's wedding ceremony.

TRANSLATION

deplorable; regrettable; disappointing

memorial day; commemoration day; anniversary

written pledge; signed note of assurance

136 怒

KUN いか.る、おこ.る

ON ド、ヌ

LEVEL TAUGHT Junior High

RADICAL 心 (忄, 小)

MEANING

Meaning: angry, be offended

EXAMPLE WORDS

怒(おこ)る

怒(いか)り

怒鳴(どな)る

EXAMPLE SENTENCE

怒(おこ)っているときは父(ちち)は何(なん)にも話(はなし)ないです

TRANSLATION

My father keeps silent when he's angry.

TRANSLATION

to get angry; to get mad,to scold

anger; rage; fury

to shout (in anger); to yell

137 怖

KUN こわ.い、こわ.がる、お.じる、おそ.れる

ON フ、ホ

LEVEL TAUGHT Junior High

RADICAL 心 (忄, 小)

MEANING

Meaning: dreadful, be frightened, fearful

EXAMPLE WORDS

恐怖(きょうふ)

怖(こわ)い

怖(こわ)い顔(かお)

EXAMPLE SENTENCE

今(いま)コロナウイルスが世界(せかい)で流行(はや)っています。とても怖(こわ)いです

TRANSLATION

The coronavirus is now prevalent all over the world. It's very scary.

TRANSLATION

fear; dread; dismay

scary; frightening

grim face; angry look

138 性

KUN	さが
ON	セイ、ショウ
LEVEL TAUGHT	G5

MEANING

Meaning: sex, gender, nature

RADICAL 心 (忄 , 㣺)

EXAMPLE WORDS

女性(じょせい)
男性(だんせい)
性別(せいべつ)

EXAMPLE SENTENCE

自分(じぶん)の性別(せいべつ)をマークして下(くだ)さい

TRANSLATION

Please indicate your gender.

TRANSLATION

woman; female; feminine gender

man; male; masculine gender

gender; distinction of sex

139 恐

KUN	おそ.れる、おそ.る、おそ.ろしい、こわ.い、こわ.がる
ON	キョウ
LEVEL TAUGHT	Junior High

MEANING

Meaning: fear, dread, awe

RADICAL 心 (忄 , 㣺)

EXAMPLE WORDS

恐怖(きょうふ)
恐縮(きょうしゅく)
恐(おそ)れる

EXAMPLE SENTENCE

私(わたし)は高(たか)い所(ところ)が恐(おそ)ろしいです

TRANSLATION

I'm terribly afraid of high places.

TRANSLATION

fear; dread; dismay

feeling obliged; being grateful

to fear; to be afraid of

140 恥

KUN	は.じる、はじ、は.じらう、は.ずかしい
ON	チ
LEVEL TAUGHT	Junior High

MEANING

Meaning: shame, dishonor

RADICAL 心 (忄 , 㣺)

EXAMPLE WORDS

恥(は)ずかしい
恥(は)じる
恥(はじ)さらし

EXAMPLE SENTENCE

簡単(かんたん)な漢字(かんじ)のに、読(よ)めなかった、恥(は)ずかしかったです

TRANSLATION

It was embrassing that I couldn't read such a simple Kanji.

TRANSLATION

embarrassing; humiliated; shy

to feel ashamed

disgrace; shame

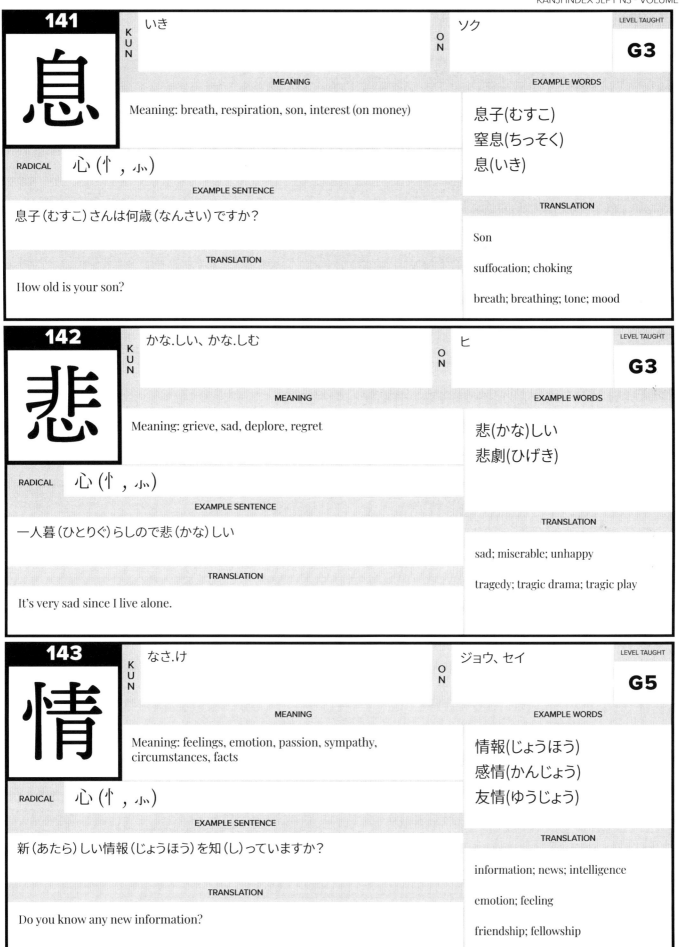

141 息

KUN いき

ON ソク

LEVEL TAUGHT G3

MEANING

Meaning: breath, respiration, son, interest (on money)

RADICAL 心 (忄 , 㣺)

EXAMPLE SENTENCE

息子(むすこ)さんは何歳(なんさい)ですか?

TRANSLATION

How old is your son?

EXAMPLE WORDS

息子(むすこ)
窒息(ちっそく)
息(いき)

TRANSLATION

Son

suffocation; choking

breath; breathing; tone; mood

142 悲

KUN かな.しい、かな.しむ

ON ヒ

LEVEL TAUGHT G3

MEANING

Meaning: grieve, sad, deplore, regret

RADICAL 心 (忄 , 㣺)

EXAMPLE SENTENCE

一人暮(ひとりぐ)らしので悲(かな)しい

TRANSLATION

It's very sad since I live alone.

EXAMPLE WORDS

悲(かな)しい
悲劇(ひげき)

TRANSLATION

sad; miserable; unhappy

tragedy; tragic drama; tragic play

143 情

KUN なさ.け

ON ジョウ、セイ

LEVEL TAUGHT G5

MEANING

Meaning: feelings, emotion, passion, sympathy, circumstances, facts

RADICAL 心 (忄 , 㣺)

EXAMPLE SENTENCE

新(あたら)しい情報(じょうほう)を知(し)っていますか?

TRANSLATION

Do you know any new information?

EXAMPLE WORDS

情報(じょうほう)
感情(かんじょう)
友情(ゆうじょう)

TRANSLATION

information; news; intelligence

emotion; feeling

friendship; fellowship

144 想

KUN おも.う
ON ソウ、ソ
LEVEL TAUGHT G3

MEANING

Meaning: concept, think, idea, thought

RADICAL 心 (忄, ⺗)

EXAMPLE SENTENCE

理想(りそう)な男性(だんせい)を探(さが)す

TRANSLATION

I'll look for the ideal man.

EXAMPLE WORDS

理想(りそう)
連想(れんそう)
空想(くうそう)

TRANSLATION

ideal; ideals

association (of ideas); being reminded (of something)

daydream; fantasy

145 愛

KUN いと.しい、かな.しい、め.でる、お.しむ、まな
ON アイ
LEVEL TAUGHT G4

MEANING

Meaning: love, affection, favourite

RADICAL 心 (忄, ⺗)

EXAMPLE SENTENCE

可愛(かわい)いペットを飼(か)いたいです

TRANSLATION

I want to keep a cute pet.

EXAMPLE WORDS

可愛(かわい)い
愛(あい)
愛想(あいそ)

TRANSLATION

cute; adorable; charming

love; affection

amiability; friendliness

146 感

KUN
ON カン
LEVEL TAUGHT G3

MEANING

Meaning: emotion, feeling, sensation

RADICAL 心 (忄, ⺗)

EXAMPLE SENTENCE

今(いま)、たくさん人(ひと)は新(あたら)しい病気(びょうき)を感染(かんせん)している

TRANSLATION

There are a lot of people presently infected with a new disease.

EXAMPLE WORDS

感情(かんじょう)
感覚(かんかく)
感染(かんせん)

TRANSLATION

emotion; feeling; feelings

sense; sensation

infection; contagion

147 慣

KUN: な.れる、な.らす
ON: カン
LEVEL TAUGHT: G5

RADICAL: 心 (忄 , ⺗)

MEANING
Meaning: accustomed, get used to, become experienced

EXAMPLE WORDS
習慣(しゅうかん)
慣(な)れる
慣例 (かんれい)

EXAMPLE SENTENCE
日本(にほん)の生活(せいかつ)に慣(な)れましたか？

TRANSLATION
Have you gotten used to life in Japan?

TRANSLATION
habit

to get used to; to grow accustomed to

custom; practice; convention

148 成

KUN: な.る、な.す、-な.す
ON: セイ、ジョウ
LEVEL TAUGHT: G4

RADICAL: 戈

MEANING
Meaning: turn into, become, get, grow, elapse, reach

EXAMPLE WORDS
成(な)る
成人(せいじん)
成(な)るべく

EXAMPLE SENTENCE
今日(きょう)のタスクを完成(かんせい)しましたか？

TRANSLATION
Have you completed today's task?

TRANSLATION
to become; to get; to grow; to be

adult (esp. person 20 years old or over); grownup

as (much) as possible; as (much) as one can

149 戦

KUN: いくさ、たたか.う、おのの.く、そよ.ぐ、わなな.く
ON: セン
LEVEL TAUGHT: G4

RADICAL: 戈

MEANING
Meaning: war, battle, match

EXAMPLE WORDS
戦争(せんそう)
戦闘(せんとう)
戦術(せんじゅつ)

EXAMPLE SENTENCE
今日(きょう)は決勝戦(けっしょうせん)がある

TRANSLATION
Today is the final match.

TRANSLATION
war

battle; fight; combat

tactics

150 戻

KUN: もど.す、もど.る

ON: レイ

Junior High

RADICAL: 戸 (戸, 戸)

MEANING
Meaning: re-, return, revert, resume, restore, go backwards

EXAMPLE SENTENCE
いつ日本(にほん)へ戻(もど)りますか?

TRANSLATION
When will you return to Japan?

EXAMPLE WORDS
戻(もど)る
戻(もど)す
払(はら)い戻(もど)す

TRANSLATION
to turn back, to return; to go back

to put back; to return

to repay; to pay back

---

151 所

KUN: ところ、-ところ、どころ、とこ

ON: ショ

G3

RADICAL: 戸 (戸, 戸)

MEANING
Meaning: place, extent

EXAMPLE SENTENCE
台所(だいどころ)はきれいですね

TRANSLATION
What a beautiful kitchen.

EXAMPLE WORDS
台所(だいどころ)
住所(じゅうしょ)
所(ところ)

TRANSLATION
kitchen

address (e.g. of house); residence

place; spot

---

152 才

KUN:

ON: サイ

G2

RADICAL: 手 (扌 龵)

MEANING
Meaning: genius, years old, cubic shaku

EXAMPLE SENTENCE
あの子(こ)は音楽(おんがく)の才能(さいのう)がある

TRANSLATION
That child has talent in music.

EXAMPLE WORDS
天才(てんさい)
才能(さいのう)
才子佳人(さいしかじん)

TRANSLATION
genius; prodigy; natural gift

talent; ability

talented man and a beautiful woman; well-matched pair

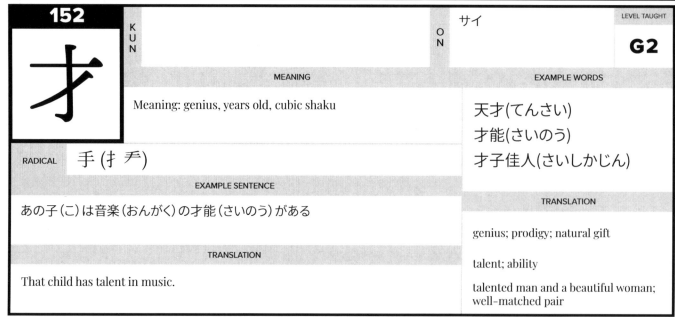

153 打

KUN う.つ、う.ち-、ぶ.つ

ON ダ、ダース

LEVEL TAUGHT G3

RADICAL 手 (扌 龵)

MEANING
Meaning: strike, hit, knock, pound, dozen

EXAMPLE WORDS
打(う)つ
打(う)ち合(あ)わせ
打(う)ち込(こ)む

EXAMPLE SENTENCE
壁(かべ)にボールを打(う)った

TRANSLATION
I hit the ball to the wall.

TRANSLATION
to hit; to strike; to to beat

advance arrangements; preparatory meeting

to drive in (e.g. nail, stake); to hammer in

---

154 払

KUN はら.う、-はら.い、-ばら.い

ON フツ、ヒツ、ホツ

LEVEL TAUGHT Junior High

RADICAL 手 (扌 龵)

MEANING
Meaning: pay, clear out, prune, banish, dispose of

EXAMPLE WORDS
払(はら)う
支払(しはら)う
支払(しはら)い

EXAMPLE SENTENCE
電気代(でんきだい)を払(はら)います

TRANSLATION
I will pay the electricity bill.

TRANSLATION
to pay (e.g. money, bill)

to pay

payment

---

155 投

KUN な.げる、-な.げ

ON トウ

LEVEL TAUGHT G3

RADICAL 手 (扌 龵)

MEANING
Meaning: throw, discard, abandon, launch into, join, invest in, hurl, give up, sell at a loss

EXAMPLE WORDS
投票(とうひょう)
投資(とうし)
投(な)げる

EXAMPLE SENTENCE
ボールを投(な)げろ

TRANSLATION
Throw the ball.

TRANSLATION
voting; poll

investment

to throw; to hurl; to fling

156

折

KUN: お.る、おり、お.り、-お.り、お.れる
ON: セツ、シャク

LEVEL TAUGHT
G4

MEANING

Meaning: fold, break, fracture, bend, yield, submit

RADICAL: 手 (扌 龵)

EXAMPLE WORDS

骨折 (こっせつ)
折 (お) る
折 (お) れる

EXAMPLE SENTENCE

折り紙 (おりがみ) はとても面白 (おもしろ) いです

TRANSLATION

Origami is quite fascinating.

TRANSLATION

bone fracture

to break; to fracture

to be broken; to snap

157

抜

KUN: ぬ.く、-ぬ.く、ぬ.き、ぬ.ける、ぬ.かす、ぬ.かる
ON: バツ、ハツ、ハイ

LEVEL TAUGHT
Junior High

MEANING

Meaning: slip out, extract, pull out, pilfer, quote, remove, omit

RADICAL: 手 (扌 龵)

EXAMPLE WORDS

抜 (ぬ) く
抜 (ぬ) ける
抜 (ぬ) け出 (だ) す

EXAMPLE SENTENCE

玉 (たま) ねぎを抜 (ぬ) いてください

TRANSLATION

Please remove the onions.

TRANSLATION

to pull out; to draw out; to extract

to come out; to fall out

to slip out; to sneak away; to break free

158

抱

KUN: だ.く、いだ.く、かか.える
ON: ホウ

LEVEL TAUGHT
Junior High

MEANING

Meaning: embrace, hug, hold in arms

RADICAL: 手 (扌 龵)

EXAMPLE WORDS

抱 (かか) える
抱 (いだ) く
辛抱 (しんぼう)

EXAMPLE SENTENCE

母 (はは) を抱 (だ) きしめました

TRANSLATION

I hugged my mother tight.

TRANSLATION

to hold or carry under or in the arms

to embrace; to hug; to hold

patience; endurance

159 押

KUN お.す、お.し-、お.っ-、お.さえる、おさ.える

ON オウ

Junior High

MEANING
Meaning: push, stop, check, subdue, attach, seize, weight, shove, press, seal, do in spite of

RADICAL 手 (扌 龵)

EXAMPLE WORDS
押(お)し入(い)れ
押(お)す
押(お)さえる

EXAMPLE SENTENCE
ボタンを押(お)しました

TRANSLATION
I pressed the button.

TRANSLATION
closet

to push; to press

to pin down; to hold down

---

160 招

KUN まね.く

ON ショウ

LEVEL TAUGHT
G5

MEANING
Meaning: beckon, invite, summon, engage

RADICAL 手 (扌 龵)

EXAMPLE WORDS
呼(よ)ぶ
招待(しょうたい)
招(まね)く

EXAMPLE SENTENCE
お客様(きゃくさま)を忘年会(ぼうねんかい)に招待(しょうたい)します

TRANSLATION
I will invite the customer to the year-end party.

TRANSLATION
to call out (to); to call; to invite

invitation

to invite; to ask

---

161 指

KUN ゆび、さ.す、-さ.し

ON シ

LEVEL TAUGHT
G3

MEANING
Meaning: finger, point to, indicate, put into, play (chess), measure (ruler)

RADICAL 手 (扌 龵)

EXAMPLE WORDS
指(ゆび)
指輪(ゆびわ)
親指(おやゆび)

EXAMPLE SENTENCE
あの指輪(ゆびわ)きれいですね

TRANSLATION
That ring is beautiful, isn't it?

TRANSLATION
finger; toe; digit

(finger) ring

thumb

162 捕

KUN と.らえる、と.らわれる、と.る、とら.える、とら.われ る、つか.まえる、つか.まる

ON ホ

LEVEL TAUGHT Junior High

RADICAL 手 (扌 龵)

MEANING
Meaning: catch, capture

EXAMPLE WORDS
逮捕(たいほ)
捕虜(ほりょ)
捕鯨(ほげい)

EXAMPLE SENTENCE
警察(けいさつ)は泥棒(どろぼう)を捕(つか)まりました

TRANSLATION
The police caught the thief.

TRANSLATION
arrest; apprehension; capture

prisoner (of war)

whaling; whale hunting

---

163 掛

KUN か.ける、-か.ける、か.け、-か.け、-が.け、か.かる、 -か.かる、-が.かる、か.かり、-が.かり、かかり、-が かり

ON カイ、ケイ

LEVEL TAUGHT Junior High

RADICAL 手 (扌 龵)

MEANING
Meaning: hang, suspend, depend, arrive at, tax, pour

EXAMPLE WORDS
掛(か)ける
掛け算(かざん)
掛(かけ)かる

EXAMPLE SENTENCE
かぎを掛(か)けてください

TRANSLATION
Please lock it.

TRANSLATION
to spend (time, money); to put on

multiplication

to take (a resource, e.g. time or money)

---

164 探

KUN さぐ.る、さが.す

ON タン

LEVEL TAUGHT G6

RADICAL 手 (扌 龵)

MEANING
Meaning: grope, search, look for

EXAMPLE WORDS
探(さが)す
探検(たんけん)
探(さぐ)る

EXAMPLE SENTENCE
仕事(しごと)を探(さが)しています

TRANSLATION
i'm looking for a job.

TRANSLATION
to search for; to look for

exploration; expedition

to feel around for; to fumble for

165 支

KUN: ささ.える、つか.える、か.う
ON: シ
LEVEL TAUGHT: G5

RADICAL: 支

MEANING
Meaning: branch, support, sustain, branch radical (no. 65)

EXAMPLE WORDS
支配(しはい)
支度(したく)
支店(してん)

TRANSLATION
domination; rule; control

preparation; arrangements

branch office; branch store

EXAMPLE SENTENCE
来月(らいげつ),支社(ししゃ)に出張(しゅっちょう)する

TRANSLATION
I will go to the company branch office for a business trip next month.

166 放

KUN: はな.す、-っぱな.し、はな.つ、はな.れる、こ.く、ほう.る
ON: ホウ
LEVEL TAUGHT: G3

RADICAL: 支

MEANING
Meaning: set free, release, fire, shoot, emit, banish, liberate

EXAMPLE WORDS
放送(ほうそう)
解放(かいほう)
放射(ほうしゃ)

TRANSLATION
broadcast; broadcasting

release; unleashing

radiation; emission

EXAMPLE SENTENCE
現場(げんば)から生放送(なまほうそう)します

TRANSLATION
This is broadcast live from the actual scene.

167 政

KUN: まつりごと、まん
ON: セイ、ショウ
LEVEL TAUGHT: G5

RADICAL: 攴 (攵)

MEANING
Meaning: politics, government

EXAMPLE WORDS
政治(せいじ)
政府(せいふ)
政党(せいとう)

TRANSLATION
politics; government

government; administration

political party

EXAMPLE SENTENCE
政府(せいふ)は新(あたら)しい法律(ほうりつ)をします

TRANSLATION
The government will make a new law.

168

敗

KUN やぶ.れる

ON ハイ

LEVEL TAUGHT
G4

MEANING

Meaning: failure, defeat, reversal

RADICAL 攴 (攵)

EXAMPLE WORDS

失敗(しっぱい)
腐敗(ふはい)
敗戦(はいせん)

EXAMPLE SENTENCE

試験(しけん)を失敗(しっぱい)しました

TRANSLATION

I failed the exam.

TRANSLATION

failure; mistake; blunder

decomposition; putrefaction

defeat; lost battle

169

散

KUN ち.る、ち.らす、-ち.らす、ち.らかす、ち.らかる、ち.らばる、ばら、ばら.ける

ON サン

LEVEL TAUGHT
G4

MEANING

Meaning: scatter, disperse, spend, squander

RADICAL 攴 (攵)

EXAMPLE WORDS

散歩(さんぽ)
拡散(かくさん)
散(ち)らかる

EXAMPLE SENTENCE

桜(さくら)の花(はな)びらのが散(ち)っている

TRANSLATION

The cherry blossoms are falling.

TRANSLATION

walk; stroll

scattering; diffusion

to be in disorder; to lie scattered around

170

数

KUN かず、かぞ.える、しばしば、せ.める、わずらわ.しい

ON スウ、ス、サク、ソク、シュ

LEVEL TAUGHT
G2

MEANING

Meaning: number, strength, fate, law, figures

RADICAL 攴 (攵)

EXAMPLE WORDS

数学(すうがく)
数字(すうじ)
数個(すうこ)

EXAMPLE SENTENCE

数学(すうがく)が苦手(にがて)です

TRANSLATION

I'm not good at Math.

TRANSLATION

mathematics; arithmetic

numeral; figure

several (objects, usu. from two to six)

171 断

KUN た.つ、ことわ.る、さだ.める

ON ダン

G5

MEANING

Meaning: severance, decline, refuse, apologize, warn, dismiss, prohibit, decision, judgement, cutting

RADICAL 斤

EXAMPLE WORDS

診断(しんだん)
判断(はんだん)
断(ことわ)る

EXAMPLE SENTENCE

招待(しょうたい)を断(ことわ)ってください

TRANSLATION

Please decline the invitation.

TRANSLATION

diagnosis; medical examination

judgement; decision

to refuse; to reject

---

172 易

KUN やさ.しい、やす.い

ON エキ、イ

G5

MEANING

Meaning: easy, ready to, simple, fortune-telling, divination

RADICAL 日

EXAMPLE WORDS

貿易(ぼうえき)
易(やす)い
容易(ようい)

EXAMPLE SENTENCE

易(やさ)しい言葉(ことば)を使(つか)います

TRANSLATION

I use simple words.

TRANSLATION

trade (foreign); international trade

easy

easy; simple; plain

---

173 昔

KUN むかし

ON セキ、シャク

G3

MEANING

Meaning: once upon a time, antiquity, old times

RADICAL 日

EXAMPLE WORDS

昔(むかし)
昔話(むかしばなし)
大昔(おおむかし)

EXAMPLE SENTENCE

これは子供(こども)の昔話(むかしばなし)です

TRANSLATION

This is a fairy tale for children.

TRANSLATION

olden days; former

old tale; folk tale

long ago; great antiquity; old-fashioned

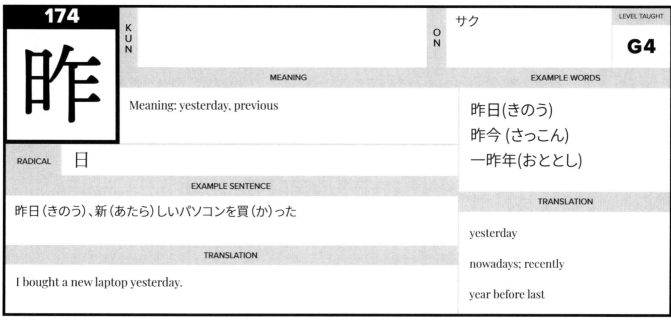

174 昨

KUN

ON サク

LEVEL TAUGHT **G4**

MEANING

Meaning: yesterday, previous

RADICAL 日

EXAMPLE WORDS

昨日(きのう)
昨今 (さっこん)
一昨年(おととし)

EXAMPLE SENTENCE

昨日(きのう)、新(あたら)しいパソコンを買(か)った

TRANSLATION

yesterday

nowadays; recently

year before last

TRANSLATION

I bought a new laptop yesterday.

175 晩

KUN

ON バン

LEVEL TAUGHT **G6**

MEANING

Meaning: nightfall, night

RADICAL 日

EXAMPLE WORDS

晩御飯(ばんごはん)
晩(ばん)
毎晩(まいばん)

EXAMPLE SENTENCE

毎晩(まいばん)、日本語(にほんご)を勉強(べんきょう)します

TRANSLATION

dinner; evening meal

evening; night

every night

TRANSLATION

I study Japanese every night.

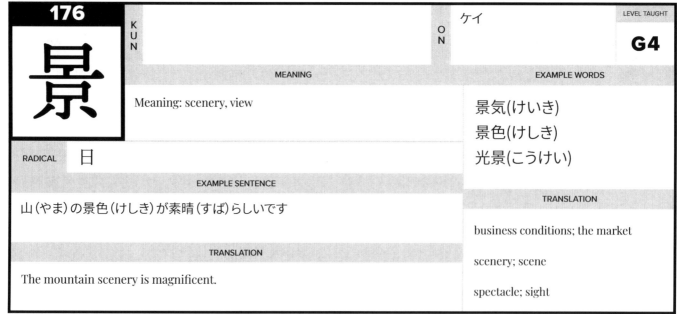

176 景

KUN

ON ケイ

LEVEL TAUGHT **G4**

MEANING

Meaning: scenery, view

RADICAL 日

EXAMPLE WORDS

景気(けいき)
景色(けしき)
光景(こうけい)

EXAMPLE SENTENCE

山(やま)の景色(けしき)が素晴(すば)らしいです

TRANSLATION

business conditions; the market

scenery; scene

spectacle; sight

TRANSLATION

The mountain scenery is magnificent.

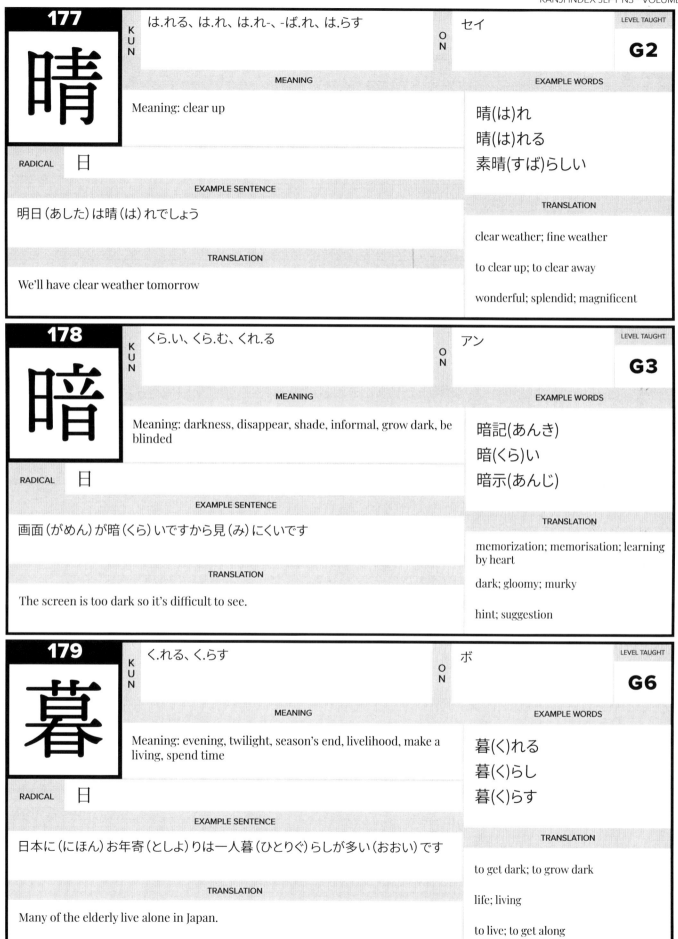

177 晴

KUN は.れる、は.れ、は.れ-、-ば.れ、は.らす

ON セイ

LEVEL TAUGHT G2

RADICAL 日

MEANING

Meaning: clear up

EXAMPLE WORDS

晴(は)れ
晴(は)れる
素晴(すば)らしい

EXAMPLE SENTENCE

明日(あした)は晴(は)れでしょう

TRANSLATION

We'll have clear weather tomorrow

TRANSLATION

clear weather; fine weather

to clear up; to clear away

wonderful; splendid; magnificent

---

178 暗

KUN くら.い、くら.む、くれ.る

ON アン

LEVEL TAUGHT G3

RADICAL 日

MEANING

Meaning: darkness, disappear, shade, informal, grow dark, be blinded

EXAMPLE WORDS

暗記(あんき)
暗(くら)い
暗示(あんじ)

EXAMPLE SENTENCE

画面(がめん)が暗(くら)いですから見(み)にくいです

TRANSLATION

The screen is too dark so it's difficult to see.

TRANSLATION

memorization; memorisation; learning by heart

dark; gloomy; murky

hint; suggestion

---

179 暮

KUN く.れる、く.らす

ON ボ

LEVEL TAUGHT G6

RADICAL 日

MEANING

Meaning: evening, twilight, season's end, livelihood, make a living, spend time

EXAMPLE WORDS

暮(く)れる
暮(く)らし
暮(く)らす

EXAMPLE SENTENCE

日本に(にほん)お年寄(としよ)りは一人暮(ひとりぐ)らしが多い(おおい)です

TRANSLATION

Many of the elderly live alone in Japan.

TRANSLATION

to get dark; to grow dark

life; living

to live; to get along

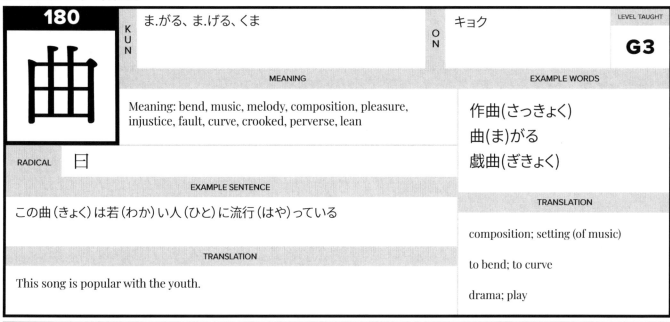

180 曲

KUN: ま.がる、ま.げる、くま
ON: キョク
LEVEL TAUGHT: G3

MEANING
Meaning: bend, music, melody, composition, pleasure, injustice, fault, curve, crooked, perverse, lean

RADICAL: 日

EXAMPLE WORDS
作曲(さっきょく)
曲(ま)がる
戯曲(ぎきょく)

EXAMPLE SENTENCE
この曲(きょく)は若(わか)い人(ひと)に流行(はや)っている

TRANSLATION
This song is popular with the youth.

TRANSLATION
composition; setting (of music)
to bend; to curve
drama; play

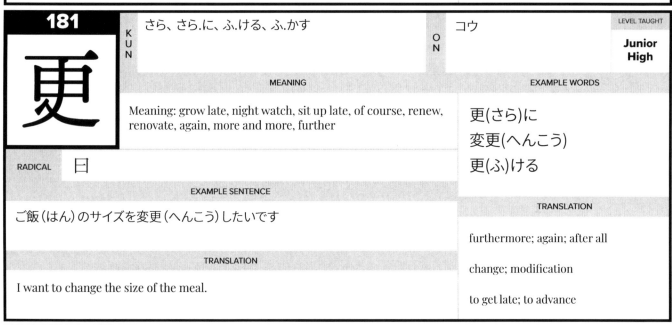

181 更

KUN: さら、さら.に、ふ.ける、ふ.かす
ON: コウ
LEVEL TAUGHT: Junior High

MEANING
Meaning: grow late, night watch, sit up late, of course, renew, renovate, again, more and more, further

RADICAL: 日

EXAMPLE WORDS
更(さら)に
変更(へんこう)
更(ふ)ける

EXAMPLE SENTENCE
ご飯(はん)のサイズを変更(へんこう)したいです

TRANSLATION
I want to change the size of the meal.

TRANSLATION
furthermore; again; after all
change; modification
to get late; to advance

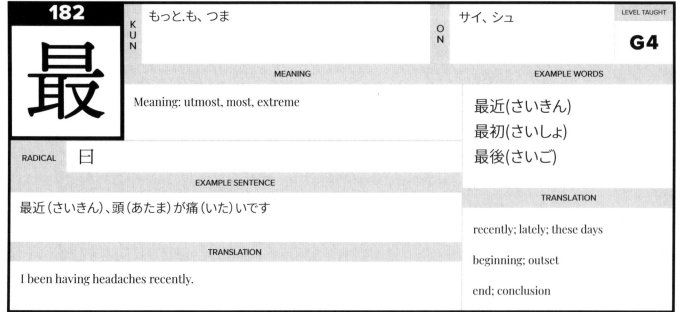

182 最

KUN: もっと.も、つま
ON: サイ、シュ
LEVEL TAUGHT: G4

MEANING
Meaning: utmost, most, extreme

RADICAL: 日

EXAMPLE WORDS
最近(さいきん)
最初(さいしょ)
最後(さいご)

EXAMPLE SENTENCE
最近(さいきん)、頭(あたま)が痛(いた)いです

TRANSLATION
I been having headaches recently.

TRANSLATION
recently; lately; these days
beginning; outset
end; conclusion

183 望

KUN のぞ.む、もち
ON ボウ、モウ
LEVEL TAUGHT G4

RADICAL 月

MEANING

Meaning: ambition, full moon, hope, desire, aspire to, expect

EXAMPLE WORDS

希望(きぼう)
望遠鏡(ぼうえんきょう)
望(のぞ)む

EXAMPLE SENTENCE

ご希望(きぼう)給料(きゅうりょう)はいくらですか?

TRANSLATION

How much is your desired of the salary?

TRANSLATION

hope; wish; aspiration

telescope

to desire

184 期

KUN
ON キ、ゴ
LEVEL TAUGHT G3

RADICAL 月

MEANING

Meaning: period, time, date, term

EXAMPLE WORDS

期待(きたい)
学期(がっき)
延期(えんき)

EXAMPLE SENTENCE

両親(りょうしん)は子供(こども)に期待(きたい)する

TRANSLATION

Parents expect from their children.

TRANSLATION

expectation; anticipation; hope

school term; semester

postponement; deferment

185 未

KUN いま.だ、ま.だ、ひつじ
ON ミ、ビ
LEVEL TAUGHT G4

RADICAL 木

MEANING

Meaning: un-, not yet, hitherto, still, even now, sign of the ram, 1-3PM, eighth sign of Chinese zodiac

EXAMPLE WORDS

未来(みらい)
未満(みまん)
未定(みてい)

EXAMPLE SENTENCE

未来(みらい)はどうなるとはだれでも知(し)りませんです

TRANSLATION

Nobody knows what the future holds.

TRANSLATION

the future (usually distant)

less than; insufficient

not yet fixed; undecided; pending

186

末

KUN すえ、うら、うれ

ON マツ、バツ

LEVEL TAUGHT G4

RADICAL 木

MEANING

Meaning: end, close, tip, powder, posterity

EXAMPLE SENTENCE

彼（かれ）は末っ子（すえっこ）です

TRANSLATION

He is the youngest child.

EXAMPLE WORDS

粗末（そまつ）
月末（げつまつ）
末（すえ）っ子（こ）

TRANSLATION

crude; rough; plain

end of the month

youngest child

187

束

KUN たば、たば.ねる、つか、つか.ねる

ON ソク

LEVEL TAUGHT G4

RADICAL 木

MEANING

Meaning: bundle, sheaf, ream, tie in bundles, govern, manage, control

EXAMPLE SENTENCE

約束（やくそく）がありますので、お先（さき）に失礼（しつれい）します

TRANSLATION

Please excuse me, I'll go ahead as I have an appointment.

EXAMPLE WORDS

約束（やくそく）
束（たば）
拘束（こうそく）

TRANSLATION

promise; agreement; arrangement

bundle; bunch

restriction; restraint

188

杯

KUN さかずき

ON ハイ

LEVEL TAUGHT Junior High

RADICAL 木

MEANING

Meaning: counter for cupfuls, wine glass, glass, toast

EXAMPLE SENTENCE

卒業！（そつぎょう）おめでとう、乾杯（かんぱい）！

TRANSLATION

Congratulations on your graduation, cheers!

EXAMPLE WORDS

乾杯（かんぱい）
一（いっ）杯（ぱい）
精一杯（せいいっぱい）

TRANSLATION

cheers; bottoms-up; prosit

full; fully; to capacity

the best one can do; one's best effort

189 果

KUN: は.たす、はた.す、-は.たす、は.てる、-は.てる、は.て

ON: カ

LEVEL TAUGHT: G4

RADICAL: 木

MEANING
Meaning: fruit, reward, carry out, achieve, complete, end, finish, succeed

EXAMPLE WORDS
結果(けっか)
果物(くだもの)
果実(かじつ)

EXAMPLE SENTENCE
結果(けっか)が未(ま)だ出(で)ていません

TRANSLATION
The results aren't out yet.

TRANSLATION
result; consequence; outcome

fruit

nut; berry

190 格

KUN:

ON: カク、コウ、キャク、ゴウ

LEVEL TAUGHT: G5

RADICAL: 木

MEANING
Meaning: status, rank, capacity, character, case (law, grammar)

EXAMPLE WORDS
価格(かかく)
資格(しかく)
人格(じんかく)

EXAMPLE SENTENCE
今(いま)、日本(にほん)に在留資格(ざいりゅうしかく)は何(なん)ですか?

TRANSLATION
What is your residence status in Japan now?

TRANSLATION
price; value; cost

qualifications; requirements

personality; character

191 構

KUN: かま.える、かま.う

ON: コウ

LEVEL TAUGHT: G5

RADICAL: 木

MEANING
Meaning: posture, build, pretend

EXAMPLE WORDS
結構(けっこう)
構(かま)う
構成(こうせい)

EXAMPLE SENTENCE
結構(けっこう)です。ありがとうございます。

TRANSLATION
No, I'm okay. Thank you very much.

TRANSLATION
splendid; nice; wonderful

to mind; to care about

composition; construction

192 様

KUN	さま、さん
ON	ヨウ、ショウ
LEVEL TAUGHT	G3

RADICAL 木

MEANING

Meaning: Esq., way, manner, situation, polite suffix

EXAMPLE WORDS

王様(おうさま)
模様(もよう)
様々(さまざま)

EXAMPLE SENTENCE

お客様(きゃくさま)、お待(ま)たせいたしました

TRANSLATION

I'm sorry for making you wait, Sir/Ma'am.

TRANSLATION

king

pattern; figure; design

various; diverse; all sorts of

193 権

KUN	おもり、かり、はか.る
ON	ケン、ゴン
LEVEL TAUGHT	G6

RADICAL 木

MEANING

Meaning: authority, power, rights

EXAMPLE WORDS

権利(けんり)
権力(けんりょく)
権威(けんい)

EXAMPLE SENTENCE

校長先生(こうちょうせんせい)は学校(がっこう)の一番(いちばん)権力(けんりょく)がある

TRANSLATION

The principal is the highest authority in school.

TRANSLATION

right; privilege

(political) power; authority

influence

194 横

KUN	よこ
ON	オウ
LEVEL TAUGHT	G3

RADICAL 木

MEANING

Meaning: sideways, side, horizontal, width, woof, unreasonable, perverse

EXAMPLE WORDS

横(よこ)
横断(おうだん)
横切(よこぎ)る

EXAMPLE SENTENCE

横断歩道(おうだんほどう)を歩(ある)きます

TRANSLATION

I will walk on the pedestrian crossing.

TRANSLATION

sideways

crossing; traversing

to cross

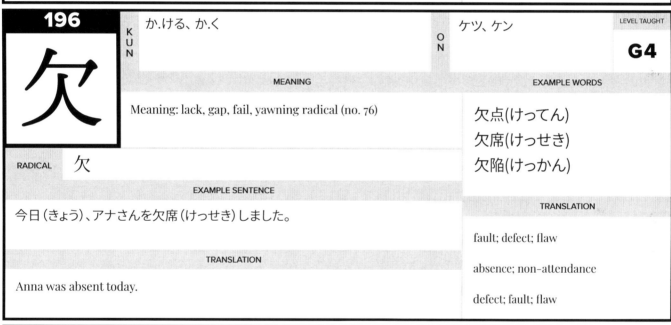

195

機

KUN はた

ON キ

LEVEL TAUGHT **G4**

RADICAL 木

MEANING

Meaning: loom, mechanism, machine, airplane, opportunity, potency, efficacy, occasion

EXAMPLE WORDS

飛行機(ひこうき)
機械(きかい)
機関(きかん)車(しゃ)

EXAMPLE SENTENCE

飛行機(ひこうき)で大阪(おおさか)へ行(い)きます

TRANSLATION

I'm going to Osaka by plane.

TRANSLATION

aeroplane; airplane; aircraft

machine; mechanism

locomotive; engine

196

欠

KUN か.ける、か.く

ON ケツ、ケン

LEVEL TAUGHT **G4**

RADICAL 欠

MEANING

Meaning: lack, gap, fail, yawning radical (no. 76)

EXAMPLE WORDS

欠点(けってん)
欠席(けっせき)
欠陥(けっかん)

EXAMPLE SENTENCE

今日(きょう)、アナさんを欠席(けっせき)しました。

TRANSLATION

Anna was absent today.

TRANSLATION

fault; defect; flaw

absence; non-attendance

defect; fault; flaw

197

次

KUN つ.ぐ、つぎ

ON ジ、シ

LEVEL TAUGHT **G3**

RADICAL 欠

MEANING

Meaning: next, order, sequence

EXAMPLE WORDS

次第(しだい)
次々(つぎつぎ)
次(つ)ぐ

EXAMPLE SENTENCE

次々(つぎつぎ)困(こま)ることを解決(かいけつ)する

TRANSLATION

I will solve the problems one by one.

TRANSLATION

depending on

in succession; one by one

to rank next to; to come after

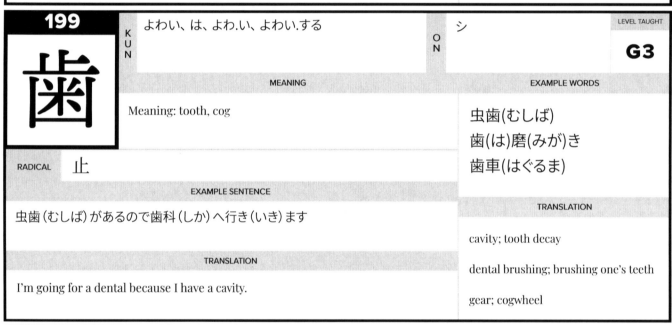

198 欲

KUN ほっ.する、ほ.しい

ON ヨク

LEVEL TAUGHT G6

RADICAL 欠

MEANING
Meaning: longing, covetousness, greed, passion, desire, craving

EXAMPLE WORDS
食欲(しょくよく)
欲(ほ)しい
欲張(よくば)り

EXAMPLE SENTENCE
今(いま)、食欲(しょくよく)がありますか？

TRANSLATION
Do you have any appetite now?

TRANSLATION
appetite (for food)

wanted; wished for; in need of; desired

greed; avarice; greedy person

---

199 歯

KUN よわい、は、よわ.い、よわい.する

ON シ

LEVEL TAUGHT G3

RADICAL 止

MEANING
Meaning: tooth, cog

EXAMPLE WORDS
虫歯(むしば)
歯(は)磨(みが)き
歯車(はぐるま)

EXAMPLE SENTENCE
虫歯(むしば)があるので歯科(しか)へ行き(いき)ます

TRANSLATION
I'm going for a dental because I have a cavity.

TRANSLATION
cavity; tooth decay

dental brushing; brushing one's teeth

gear; cogwheel

---

200 歳

KUN とし、とせ、よわい

ON サイ、セイ

LEVEL TAUGHT Junior High

RADICAL 止

MEANING
Meaning: year-end, age, occasion, opportunity

EXAMPLE WORDS
歳(さい)
歳入(さいにゅう)
歳月(さいげつ)

EXAMPLE SENTENCE
お年寄り(としより)は65歳(さい)以上(いじょう)です

TRANSLATION
The elderly are from 65 years or older.

TRANSLATION
-years-old [suffix,counter]

annual revenue (government)

time; years

201

残

KUN のこ.る、のこ.す、そこな.う、のこ.り

ON ザン、サン

G4

MEANING

Meaning: remainder, leftover, balance

RADICAL 歹 (歺)

EXAMPLE WORDS

残念(ざんねん)
残(のこ)る
残(のこ)す

EXAMPLE SENTENCE

仕事(しごと)を残(のこ)っている

TRANSLATION

I have work left to do.

TRANSLATION

deplorable; regrettable

to remain; to be left

to leave (behind); to leave (undone); to not finish

202

段

KUN

ON ダン、タン

G6

MEANING

Meaning: grade, steps, stairs

RADICAL 殳

EXAMPLE WORDS

階段(かいだん)
段々(だんだん)
手段(しゅだん)

EXAMPLE SENTENCE

階段(かいだん)を上(のぼ)ります

TRANSLATION

I'll climb the stairs.

TRANSLATION

stairs; stairway; staircase

more and more; increasingly

means; way; measure

203

殺

KUN ころ.す、-ごろ.し、そ.ぐ

ON サツ、サイ、セツ

G5

MEANING

Meaning: kill, murder, butcher, slice off, split, diminish, reduce, spoil

RADICAL 殳

EXAMPLE WORDS

自殺(じさつ)
殺人(さつじん)
殺(ころ)す

EXAMPLE SENTENCE

東京(とうきょう)ではでは事故(じこ)の自殺(じさつ)が多い(おおい)です

TRANSLATION

There are many suicides in Tokyo.

TRANSLATION

suicide

murder; homicide

to kill

204 民

KUN: たみ
ON: ミン
LEVEL TAUGHT: G4

RADICAL: 氏

MEANING: Meaning: people, nation, subjects

EXAMPLE WORDS:
市民(しみん)
国民(こくみん)
民族(みんぞく)

TRANSLATION:
citizen; citizenry; public

people (of a country)

race; ethnic group

EXAMPLE SENTENCE:
国民(こくみん)の意見(いけん)を取(と)ります

TRANSLATION:
Take public opinion.

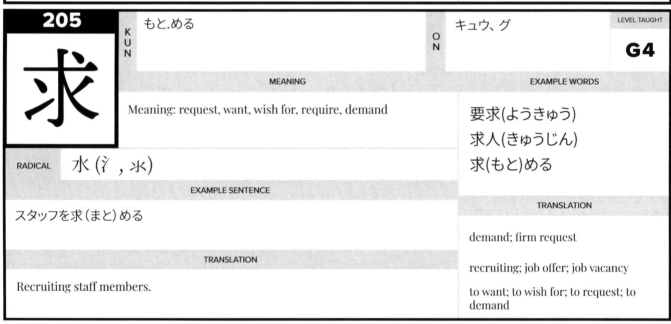

205 求

KUN: もと.める
ON: キュウ、グ
LEVEL TAUGHT: G4

RADICAL: 水 (氵, 氺)

MEANING: Meaning: request, want, wish for, require, demand

EXAMPLE WORDS:
要求(ようきゅう)
求人(きゅうじん)
求(もと)める

TRANSLATION:
demand; firm request

recruiting; job offer; job vacancy

to want; to wish for; to request; to demand

EXAMPLE SENTENCE:
スタッフを求(まと)める

TRANSLATION:
Recruiting staff members.

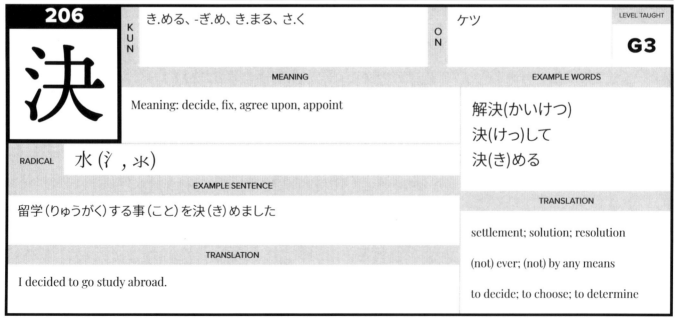

206 決

KUN: き.める、-ぎ.め、き.まる、さ.く
ON: ケツ
LEVEL TAUGHT: G3

RADICAL: 水 (氵, 氺)

MEANING: Meaning: decide, fix, agree upon, appoint

EXAMPLE WORDS:
解決(かいけつ)
決(けっ)して
決(き)める

TRANSLATION:
settlement; solution; resolution

(not) ever; (not) by any means

to decide; to choose; to determine

EXAMPLE SENTENCE:
留学(りゅうがく)する事(こと)を決(き)めました

TRANSLATION:
I decided to go study abroad.

207

治

KUN おさ.める、おさ.まる、なお.る、なお.す

ON ジ、チ

LEVEL TAUGHT **G4**

MEANING

Meaning: reign, be at peace, calm down, subdue, quell, govt, cure, heal, rule, conserve

RADICAL 水 (氵, 氺)

EXAMPLE WORDS

政治(せいじ)
自治(じち)
治療(ちりょう)

EXAMPLE SENTENCE

この病気（びょうき）は治療（ちりょう）が必要（ひつよう）です

TRANSLATION

politics; government

self-government; autonomy

(medical) treatment; care; therapy

TRANSLATION

This disease requires medical treatment.

208

法

KUN のり

ON ホウ、ハッ、ホッ、フラン

LEVEL TAUGHT **G4**

MEANING

Meaning: method, law, rule, principle, model, system

RADICAL 水 (氵, 氺)

EXAMPLE WORDS

法律(ほうりつ)
文法(ぶんぽう)
憲法(けんぽう)

EXAMPLE SENTENCE

国（くに）の法律（ほうりつ）を守（まも）る

TRANSLATION

law

grammar

constitution

TRANSLATION

I comply with the laws of the country.

209

泳

KUN およ.ぐ

ON エイ

LEVEL TAUGHT **G3**

MEANING

Meaning: swim

RADICAL 水 (氵, 氺)

EXAMPLE WORDS

水泳(すいえい)
泳(およ)ぐ
泳者(えいしゃ)

EXAMPLE SENTENCE

あなたは泳（およ）げますか？

TRANSLATION

swimming

to swim

a swimmer

TRANSLATION

Can you swim?

210 洗

KUN あら.う	**ON** セン
	LEVEL TAUGHT G6

MEANING

Meaning: wash, inquire into, probe

RADICAL 水 (氵, 氺)

EXAMPLE SENTENCE

お手洗(てあら)いはどこですか？

TRANSLATION

Where is the restroom?

EXAMPLE WORDS

洗濯(せんたく)
洗(あら)う
お手洗(てあら)い

TRANSLATION

washing; laundry

to wash; to cleanse; to rinse

toilet; restroom

211 活

KUN い.きる、い.かす、い.ける	**ON** カツ
	LEVEL TAUGHT G2

MEANING

Meaning: lively, resuscitation, being helped, living

RADICAL 水 (氵, 氺)

EXAMPLE SENTENCE

日本(にほん)の生活(せいかつ)はどうですか？

TRANSLATION

How is life in Japan?

EXAMPLE WORDS

生活(せいかつ)
活用(かつよう)

TRANSLATION

living; life, livelihood

practical use; application

212 流

KUN なが.れる、なが.れ、なが.す、-なが.す	**ON** リュウ、ル
	LEVEL TAUGHT G3

MEANING

Meaning: current, a sink, flow, forfeit

RADICAL 水 (氵, 氺)

EXAMPLE SENTENCE

音楽(おんがく)が流(なが)れます

TRANSLATION

The music plays.

EXAMPLE WORDS

流(なが)れる
交流(こうりゅう)

TRANSLATION

to be washed away; to be carried; to be heard

(cultural) exchange; (social, etc.) networking

213 浮

KUN う.く、う.かれる、う.かぶ、う.かべる

ON フ

LEVEL TAUGHT Junior High

MEANING

Meaning: floating, float, rise to surface

RADICAL 水 (氵, 氺)

EXAMPLE WORDS

浮力(ふりょく)
浮(う)かべる

EXAMPLE SENTENCE

紙(かみ)は水面(すいめん)に浮(う)きている

TRANSLATION

buoyancy; floating power

to float; to show on one's face (smile, sadness, etc.)

TRANSLATION

The paper is floating on the surface of the water.

214 消

KUN き.える、け.す

ON ショウ

LEVEL TAUGHT G3

MEANING

Meaning: extinguish, blow out, turn off, neutralize, cancel

RADICAL 水 (氵, 氺)

EXAMPLE WORDS

消費(しょうひ)
消(け)す
消(き)える

EXAMPLE SENTENCE

書(かいた)いた字(じ)を消(け)します

TRANSLATION

consumption; expenditure

to erase; to turn off (power)

to go out; to vanish; to disappear

TRANSLATION

I erased what I wrote.

215 深

KUN ふか.い、-ぶか.い、ふか.まる、ふか.める、み-

ON シン

LEVEL TAUGHT G3

MEANING

Meaning: deep, heighten, intensify, strengthen

RADICAL 水 (氵, 氺)

EXAMPLE WORDS

深夜(しんや)
深刻(しんこく)
深(ふか)い

EXAMPLE SENTENCE

海(うみ)が深(ふか)いです

TRANSLATION

late at night

serious; severe; grave; acute

deep

TRANSLATION

The sea is deep.

216

済

KUN す.む、-ず.み、-ずみ、す.まない、す.ます、-す.ます、すく.う、な.す、わたし、わた.る

ON サイ、セイ

LEVEL TAUGHT G6

RADICAL 水 (氵, 氺)

MEANING

Meaning: settle (debt, etc.), relieve (burden), finish, come to an end, excusable, need not

EXAMPLE WORDS

経済(けいざい)

救済(きゅうさい)

済(す)む

EXAMPLE SENTENCE

今年(ことし)　世界(せかい)の経済(けいざい)が良(よ)くないです

TRANSLATION

economy; economics

relief; aid; help; rescue

to finish; to end; to be completed; to feel at ease

TRANSLATION

The world's economy is not good this year.

217

渡

KUN わた.る、-わた.る、わた.す

ON ト

LEVEL TAUGHT Junior High

RADICAL 水 (氵, 氺)

MEANING

Meaning: transit, ford, ferry, cross, import, deliver, diameter, migrate

EXAMPLE WORDS

渡(わた)す

渡航(とこう)

EXAMPLE SENTENCE

友達(ともだち)に鍵(かぎ)を渡(わた)します

TRANSLATION

to ferry across; to hand over; to hand in

voyage; passage; travelling

TRANSLATION

I'll hand over the key to a friend.

218

港

KUN みなと

ON コウ

LEVEL TAUGHT G3

RADICAL 水 (氵, 氺)

MEANING

Meaning: harbor

EXAMPLE WORDS

空港(くうこう)

港(みなと)

香港(ホンコン)

EXAMPLE SENTENCE

港(みなと)へ遊(あそ)びに行(い)きます

TRANSLATION

airport

harbor; port

Hong Kong

TRANSLATION

I'm going to hangout at the harbor.

219 満

KUN み.ちる、み.つ、み.たす

ON マン、バン

LEVEL TAUGHT G4

RADICAL 水 (氵, 氺)

MEANING
Meaning: full, fullness, enough, satisfy

EXAMPLE WORDS
満月(まんげつ)
満足(まんぞく)
不満(ふまん)

EXAMPLE SENTENCE
今日(きょう)は満月(まんげつ)ですね。素敵(すてき)な月(つき)です。

TRANSLATION
It's a full moon today. The moon is so beautiful.

TRANSLATION
full moon

satisfaction; contentment

dissatisfaction; discontent

---

220 演

KUN

ON エン

LEVEL TAUGHT G5

RADICAL 水 (氵, 氺)

MEANING
Meaning: performance, act, play, render, stage

EXAMPLE WORDS
演説(えんぜつ)
演劇(えんげき)
演奏(えんそう)

EXAMPLE SENTENCE
彼(かれ)は熱演(ねつえん)している

TRANSLATION
He is performing very passionately.

TRANSLATION
speech; address

drama; theater; play

musical performance

---

221 点

KUN つ.ける、つ.く、た.てる、さ.す、とぼ.す、とも.す、ぼ ち

ON テン

LEVEL TAUGHT G2

RADICAL 火 (灬)

MEANING
Meaning: spot, point, mark, speck, decimal point

EXAMPLE WORDS
交差点(こうさてん)
頂点(ちょうてん)
終点(しゅうてん)

EXAMPLE SENTENCE
次(つぎ)駅(えき)は終点(しゅうてん)です

TRANSLATION
The next station is the last stop.

TRANSLATION
crossing; intersection

top; summit

terminus; last stop (e.g. train)

222 然

KUN しか、しか.り、しか.し、さ

ON ゼン、ネン

G4

RADICAL 火 (灬)

MEANING
Meaning: sort of thing, so, if so, in that case, well

EXAMPLE WORDS
偶然(ぐうぜん)
自然(しぜん)
然(しか)し

EXAMPLE SENTENCE
自然環境(しぜんかんきょう)を守(まも)る

TRANSLATION
We will protect the natural environment.

TRANSLATION
coincidence; chance; accident

nature

however; but

---

223 煙

KUN けむ.る、けむり、けむ.い

ON エン

Junior High

RADICAL 火 (灬)

MEANING
Meaning: smoke

EXAMPLE WORDS
煙草(たばこ)
禁煙(きんえん)
煙突(えんとつ)

EXAMPLE SENTENCE
こちらは禁煙(きんえん)なところです

TRANSLATION
This is the no-smoking area.

TRANSLATION
tobacco; cigarette

abstaining from smoking

chimney; smokestack

---

224 熱

KUN あつ.い

ON ネツ

G4

RADICAL 火 (灬)

MEANING
Meaning: heat, temperature, fever, mania, passion

EXAMPLE WORDS
熱帯(ねったい)
熱(あつ)い
熱(ねつ)

EXAMPLE SENTENCE
熱(ねつ)があります

TRANSLATION
I have a fever.

TRANSLATION
tropics

hot (thing); passionate (feelings, etc.)

fever; temperature

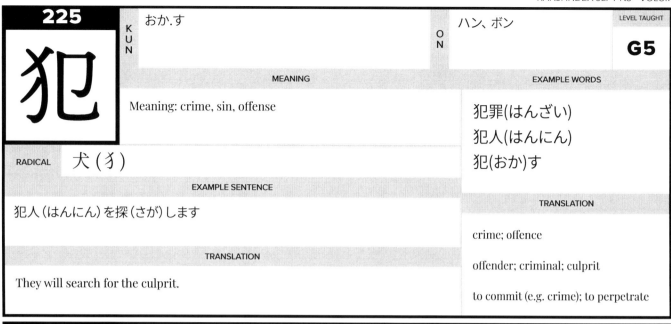

225 犯

KUN おか.す
ON ハン、ボン
LEVEL TAUGHT **G5**

MEANING
Meaning: crime, sin, offense

RADICAL 犬 (犭)

EXAMPLE WORDS
犯罪(はんざい)
犯人(はんにん)
犯(おか)す

EXAMPLE SENTENCE
犯人(はんにん)を探(さが)します

TRANSLATION
crime; offence

offender; criminal; culprit

to commit (e.g. crime); to perpetrate

TRANSLATION
They will search for the culprit.

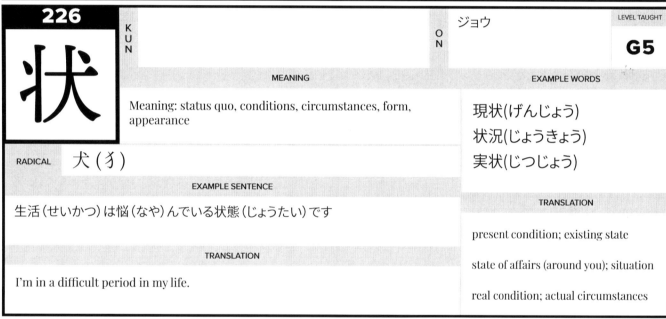

226 状

KUN
ON ジョウ
LEVEL TAUGHT **G5**

MEANING
Meaning: status quo, conditions, circumstances, form, appearance

RADICAL 犬 (犭)

EXAMPLE WORDS
現状(げんじょう)
状況(じょうきょう)
実状(じつじょう)

EXAMPLE SENTENCE
生活(せいかつ)は悩(なや)んでいる状態(じょうたい)です

TRANSLATION
present condition; existing state

state of affairs (around you); situation

real condition; actual circumstances

TRANSLATION
I'm in a difficult period in my life.

227 猫

KUN ねこ
ON ビョウ
LEVEL TAUGHT **Junior High**

MEANING
Meaning: cat

RADICAL 犬 (犭)

EXAMPLE WORDS
猫(ねこ)
猫背(ねこぜ)
猫舌(ねこじた)

EXAMPLE SENTENCE
猫(ねこ)のエサを買(か)う

TRANSLATION
cat (esp. the domestic cat)

bent back; hunchback; stoop

inability to take hot food; cat tongue

TRANSLATION
I will buy cat food

228 王

KUN

ON オウ、-ノウ

LEVEL TAUGHT G1

MEANING

Meaning: king, rule, magnate

EXAMPLE WORDS

王様(おうさま)
女王(じょおう)
王(おう)

RADICAL 玉 (王)

TRANSLATION

king (honorific)

queen

king; ruler; sovereign; monarch

EXAMPLE SENTENCE

今(いま)の時代(じだい)に子供(こども)は王様(おうさま)のようです

TRANSLATION

Children are like kings these days.

---

229 現

KUN あらわ.れる、あらわ.す、うつつ、うつ.つ

ON ゲン

LEVEL TAUGHT G5

MEANING

Meaning: present, existing, actual

EXAMPLE WORDS

現在(げんざい)
現実(げんじつ)
現金(げんきん)

RADICAL 玉 (王)

TRANSLATION

now; current; present time; as of

reality; actuality; hard fact

cash; ready money; money on hand

EXAMPLE SENTENCE

現金(げんきん)で支払(しはら)います

TRANSLATION

I will pay in cash.

---

230 球

KUN たま

ON キュウ

LEVEL TAUGHT G3

MEANING

Meaning: ball, sphere

EXAMPLE WORDS

地球(ちきゅう)
電球(でんきゅう)
球技(きゅうぎ)

RADICAL 玉 (王)

TRANSLATION

Earth; the globe

light bulb

ball game (e.g. baseball, tennis, soccer)

EXAMPLE SENTENCE

電球(でんきゅう)を換(か)える

TRANSLATION

I will change the light bulb.

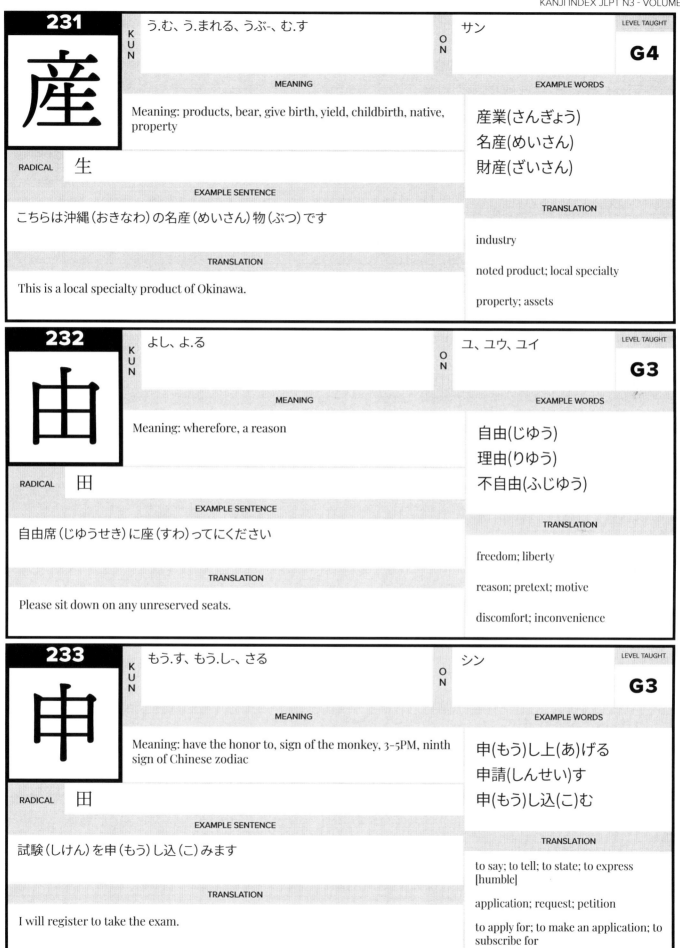

231

産

KUN: う.む、う.まれる、うぶ-、む.す

ON: サン

LEVEL TAUGHT: G4

RADICAL: 生

MEANING

Meaning: products, bear, give birth, yield, childbirth, native, property

EXAMPLE WORDS

産業(さんぎょう)
名産(めいさん)
財産(ざいさん)

EXAMPLE SENTENCE

こちらは沖縄(おきなわ)の名産(めいさん)物(ぶつ)です

TRANSLATION

This is a local specialty product of Okinawa.

TRANSLATION

industry

noted product; local specialty

property; assets

232

由

KUN: よし、よ.る

ON: ユ、ユウ、ユイ

LEVEL TAUGHT: G3

RADICAL: 田

MEANING

Meaning: wherefore, a reason

EXAMPLE WORDS

自由(じゆう)
理由(りゆう)
不自由(ふじゆう)

EXAMPLE SENTENCE

自由席(じゆうせき)に座(すわ)ってにください

TRANSLATION

Please sit down on any unreserved seats.

TRANSLATION

freedom; liberty

reason; pretext; motive

discomfort; inconvenience

233

申

KUN: もう.す、もう.し-、さる

ON: シン

LEVEL TAUGHT: G3

RADICAL: 田

MEANING

Meaning: have the honor to, sign of the monkey, 3-5PM, ninth sign of Chinese zodiac

EXAMPLE WORDS

申(もう)し上(あ)げる
申請(しんせい)す
申(もう)し込(こ)む

EXAMPLE SENTENCE

試験(しけん)を申(もう)し込(こ)みます

TRANSLATION

I will register to take the exam.

TRANSLATION

to say; to tell; to state; to express [humble]

application; request; petition

to apply for; to make an application; to subscribe for

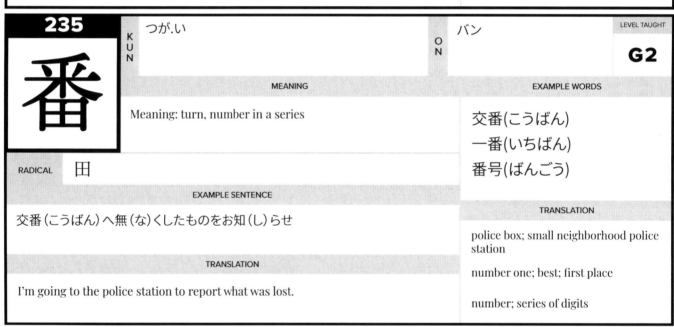

234 留

KUN と.める、と.まる、とど.める、とど.まる、るうぶる

ON リュウ、ル

LEVEL TAUGHT G5

MEANING

Meaning: detain, fasten, halt, stop

RADICAL 田

EXAMPLE WORDS

留学(りゅうがく)
留(と)まる
留学生(りゅうがくせい)

EXAMPLE SENTENCE

私(わたし)は留学生(りゅうがくせい)です

TRANSLATION

I am an overseas exchange student.

TRANSLATION

studying abroad

to stop (moving); to come to a stop

overseas student; exchange student

235 番

KUN つが.い

ON バン

LEVEL TAUGHT G2

MEANING

Meaning: turn, number in a series

RADICAL 田

EXAMPLE WORDS

交番(こうばん)
一番(いちばん)
番号(ばんごう)

EXAMPLE SENTENCE

交番(こうばん)へ無(な)くしたものをお知(し)らせ

TRANSLATION

I'm going to the police station to report what was lost.

TRANSLATION

police box; small neighborhood police station

number one; best; first place

number; series of digits

236 疑

KUN うたが.う

ON ギ

LEVEL TAUGHT G6

MEANING

Meaning: doubt, distrust, be suspicious, question

RADICAL 疋(正)

EXAMPLE WORDS

疑(うたが)う
疑問(ぎもん)

EXAMPLE SENTENCE

この問題(もんだい)はまだたくさん疑問(ぎもん)がある

TRANSLATION

This case still has a lot of questions surrounding it.

TRANSLATION

to doubt; to distrust; to be suspicious of

doubt; question; suspicion

237 疲

KUN つか.れる、-づか.れ、つか.らす

ON ヒ

LEVEL TAUGHT Junior High

RADICAL 疒

MEANING

Meaning: exhausted, tire, weary

EXAMPLE WORDS

疲(つか)れる

疲労(ひろう)

TRANSLATION

to get tired; to get fatigued

fatigue; weariness

EXAMPLE SENTENCE

お疲(つか)れ様(さま)です

TRANSLATION

You have worked hard / Thank you for the hard work.
(Expression or greeting when someone finishes work/task)

238 痛

KUN いた.い、いた.む、いた.ましい、いた.める

ON ツウ

LEVEL TAUGHT G6

RADICAL 疒

MEANING

Meaning: pain, hurt, damage, bruise

EXAMPLE WORDS

痛(いた)み

頭痛(ずつう)

痛恨(つうこん)

TRANSLATION

pain, headache, sore; grief; distress

headache

regretful; sorrowful; bitter; contrition

EXAMPLE SENTENCE

昨日(きのう)から頭痛(ずつう)です

TRANSLATION

I have a headache since yesterday.

239 登

KUN のぼ.る、あ.がる

ON トウ、ト、ドウ、ショウ、チョウ

LEVEL TAUGHT G3

RADICAL 癶

MEANING

Meaning: ascend, climb up

EXAMPLE WORDS

登山(とざん)

登場(とうじょう)

登記(とうき)

TRANSLATION

mountain climbing

entry (on stage); appearance (on screen)

registry; registration

EXAMPLE SENTENCE

今週(こんしゅう)の日曜日(にちようび)に登山(とざん)します

TRANSLATION

I'll be mountain climbing this Sunday.

240 皆

KUN みな、みんな
ON カイ
LEVEL TAUGHT Junior High

MEANING
Meaning: all, everything

RADICAL 白

EXAMPLE WORDS
皆(みんな)
皆(みな)さん

EXAMPLE SENTENCE
皆(みんな)さん、おはようございます！

TRANSLATION
Good morning everyone!

TRANSLATION
everyone; everybody; all

all; everyone; everybody [honorific]

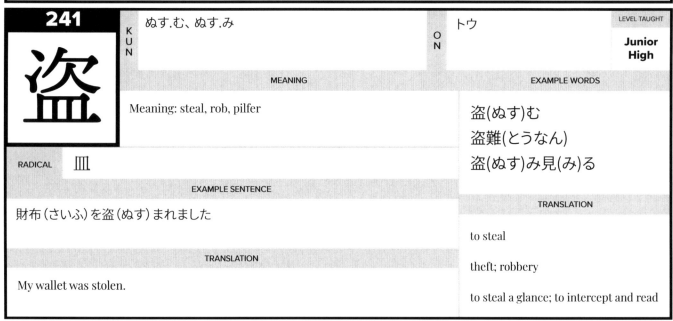

241 盗

KUN ぬす.む、ぬす.み
ON トウ
LEVEL TAUGHT Junior High

MEANING
Meaning: steal, rob, pilfer

RADICAL 皿

EXAMPLE WORDS
盗(ぬす)む
盗難(とうなん)
盗(ぬす)み見(み)る

EXAMPLE SENTENCE
財布(さいふ)を盗(ぬす)まれました

TRANSLATION
My wallet was stolen.

TRANSLATION
to steal

theft; robbery

to steal a glance; to intercept and read

242 直

KUN ただ.ちに、なお.す、-なお.す、なお.る、なお.き、す.ぐ
ON チョク、ジキ、ジカ
LEVEL TAUGHT G2

MEANING
Meaning: straightaway, honesty, frankness, fix, repair

RADICAL 目

EXAMPLE WORDS
直(じき)
直線(ちょくせん)
率直(そっちょく)

EXAMPLE SENTENCE
彼女(かのじょ)は率直(そっちょく)な人(ひと)です

TRANSLATION
She is a straightforward person.

TRANSLATION
soon; in a moment; before long; shortly

straight line

frank; candid; straightforward

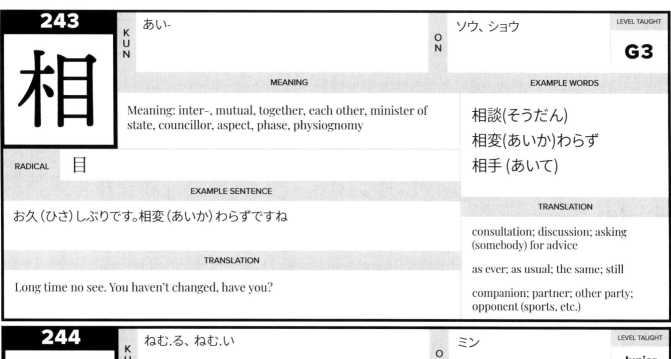

243 相

KUN あい-

ON ソウ、ショウ

LEVEL TAUGHT G3

MEANING

Meaning: inter–, mutual, together, each other, minister of state, councillor, aspect, phase, physiognomy

RADICAL 目

EXAMPLE WORDS

相談(そうだん)
相変(あいか)わらず
相手 (あいて)

EXAMPLE SENTENCE

お久(ひさ)しぶりです。相変(あいか)わらずですね

TRANSLATION

consultation; discussion; asking (somebody) for advice

as ever; as usual; the same; still

companion; partner; other party; opponent (sports, etc.)

TRANSLATION

Long time no see. You haven't changed, have you?

---

244 眠

KUN ねむ.る、ねむ.い

ON ミン

LEVEL TAUGHT Junior High

MEANING

Meaning: sleep, die, sleepy

RADICAL 目

EXAMPLE WORDS

眠(ねむ)る
眠(ねむ)い
睡眠時間(すいみんじかん)

EXAMPLE SENTENCE

睡眠時間(すいみんじかん)はどうでしょうか？

TRANSLATION

to sleep

sleepy; drowsy; somnolent

(one's) sleeping hours; hours of sleep

TRANSLATION

What about the time to sleep?

Kanji Practice Section
Worksheets

Stroke Order

123

式

Kun:

On:

Radical:

Meaning:

Words that use [式]:

Use [式] in a sentence:

1

2

3

Notes:

Stroke Order

124

引

Kun:

On:

Radical:

Meaning:

Words that use [引]:

Use [引] in a sentence:

1

2

3

Notes:

125

当

Stroke Order

Kun:

On:

Radical:

Meaning:

Words that use [当]:

Use [当] in a sentence:

1

2

3

Notes:

126

形

Stroke Order

Kun:

On:

Radical:

Meaning:

Words that use [形]:

Use [形] in a sentence:

1

2

3

Notes:

127

役

Kun:

On:

Radical:

Meaning:

Stroke Order

Words that use [役]:

Use [役] in a sentence:

1

2

3

Notes:

128

彼

Kun:

On:

Radical:

Meaning:

Stroke Order

彼

Words that use [彼]:

Use [彼] in a sentence:

1

2

3

Notes:

129

徒

Kun:

On:

Radical:

Meaning:

Stroke Order

Words that use [徒]:

Use [徒] in a sentence:

1

2

3

Notes:

130

得

Kun:

On:

Radical:

Meaning:

Stroke Order

Words that use [得]:

Use [得] in a sentence:

1

2

3

Notes:

131

御

Kun:

On:

Radical:

Meaning:

御

1 2 3 4 5 6 7 8 9 10 11 12

Stroke Order

Words that use [御]:

Use [御] in a sentence:

1

2

3

Notes:

132

必

Stroke Order

Kun:

On:

Radical:

Meaning:

Words that use [必]:

Use [必] in a sentence:

1

2

3

Notes:

133

忘

Kun:

On:

Radical:

Meaning:

Stroke Order

Words that use [忘]:

Use [忘] in a sentence:

1

2

3

Notes:

134

忙

Stroke Order

Kun:

On:

Radical:

Meaning:

Words that use [忙]:

Use [忙] in a sentence:

1

2

3

Notes:

135

念

Stroke Order

Kun:

On:

Radical:

Meaning:

Words that use [念]:

Use [念] in a sentence:

1

2

3

Notes:

136

怒

Kun:

On:

Radical:

Meaning:

Stroke Order

Words that use [怒]:

Use [怒] in a sentence:

1

2

3

Notes:

KANJI PRACTICE SECTION WORKSHEETS

137

怖

Kun:

On: Radical:

Meaning:

怖

3 4 5 1 2 8 7 6

Stroke Order

Words that use [怖]:

Use [怖] in a sentence:

1

2

3

Notes:

138

性

Stroke Order

Kun:

On:

Radical:

Meaning:

Words that use [性]:

Use [性] in a sentence:

1

2

3

Notes:

139

恐

Kun:

On:

Radical:

Meaning:

Stroke Order

Words that use [恐]:

Use [恐] in a sentence:

1

2

3

Notes:

140

恥

Kun:

On:

Radical:

Meaning:

Stroke Order

Words that use [恥]:

Use [恥] in a sentence:

1

2

3

Notes:

141

息

Stroke Order

Kun:

On:

Radical:

Meaning:

Words that use [息]:

Use [息] in a sentence:

1

2

3

Notes:

142

悲

Stroke Order

Kun:

On:

Radical:

Meaning:

Words that use [悲]:

Use [悲] in a sentence:

1

2

3

Notes:

143

情

Kun:

On:

Radical:

Meaning:

Stroke Order

Words that use [情]:

Use [情] in a sentence:

1

2

3

Notes:

144

想

Kun:

On:

Radical:

Meaning:

Stroke Order

Words that use [想]:

Use [想] in a sentence:

1

2

3

Notes:

145

愛

Stroke Order

Kun:

On:

Radical:

Meaning:

Words that use [愛]:

Use [愛] in a sentence:

1

2

3

Notes:

146

感

Kun:

On:

Radical:

Meaning:

Stroke Order

Words that use [感]:

Use [感] in a sentence:

1

2

3

Notes:

147

慣

Stroke Order

Kun:

On:

Radical:

Meaning:

Words that use [慣]:

Use [慣] in a sentence:

1

2

3

Notes:

148

成

Kun:

On:

Radical:

Meaning:

Stroke Order

Words that use [成]:

Use [成] in a sentence:

1

2

3

Notes:

KANJI PRACTICE SECTION WORKSHEETS

149

戦

Stroke Order

Kun:

On:

Radical:

Meaning:

Words that use [戦]:

Use [戦] in a sentence:

1

2

3

Notes:

JLPT N3 - VOLUME 2 - PRACTICE WORKBOOK | **79**

150

戻

Stroke Order

Kun:

On:

Radical:

Meaning:

Words that use [戻]:

Use [戻] in a sentence:

1

2

3

Notes:

Stroke Order

151

所

Kun:

On:

Radical:

Meaning:

Words that use [所]:

Use [所] in a sentence:

1

2

3

Notes:

152

才

Kun:

On:

Radical:

Meaning:

Stroke Order

Words that use [才]:

Use [才] in a sentence:

1

2

3

Notes:

153

打

Stroke Order

Kun:

On:

Radical:

Meaning:

Words that use [打]:

Use [打] in a sentence:

1

2

3

Notes:

154

払

Stroke Order

Kun:

On:

Radical:

Meaning:

Words that use [払]:

Use [払] in a sentence:

1

2

3

Notes:

155

投

Stroke Order

Kun:

On:

Radical:

Meaning:

Words that use [投]:

Use [投] in a sentence:

1

2

3

Notes:

156

折

Kun:

On:

Radical:

Meaning:

Stroke Order

Words that use [折]:

Use [折] in a sentence:

1

2

3

Notes:

157

抜

Kun:

On:

Radical:

Meaning:

Stroke Order

Words that use [抜]:

Use [抜] in a sentence:

1

2

3

Notes:

抱

Stroke Order

158

抱

Kun:

On:

Radical:

Meaning:

Words that use [抱]:

Use [抱] in a sentence:

1

2

3

Notes:

Stroke Order

159 押

Kun:

On:

Radical:

Meaning:

Words that use [押]:

Use [押] in a sentence:

1

2

3

Notes:

160

招

Kun:

On:

Radical:

Meaning:

Stroke Order

Words that use [招]:

Use [招] in a sentence:

1

2

3

Notes:

161

指

Stroke Order

Kun:

On:

Radical:

Meaning:

Words that use [指]:

Use [指] in a sentence:

1

2

3

Notes:

162

捕

Kun:

On:

Radical:

Meaning:

Stroke Order

Words that use [捕]:

Use [捕] in a sentence:

1

2

3

Notes:

163

掛

Kun:

On:

Radical:

Meaning:

Stroke Order

Words that use [掛]:

Use [掛] in a sentence:

1

2

3

Notes:

164

探

Kun:

On:

Radical:

Meaning:

Stroke Order

Words that use [探]:

Use [探] in a sentence:

1

2

3

Notes:

支

Stroke Order

165

支

Kun:

On:

Radical:

Meaning:

Words that use [支]:

Use [支] in a sentence:

1

2

3

Notes:

166

放

Kun:

On:

Radical:

Meaning:

Stroke Order

Words that use [放]:

Use [放] in a sentence:

1

2

3

Notes:

167

政

Kun:

On:

Radical:

Meaning:

Stroke Order

Words that use [政]:

Use [政] in a sentence:

1

2

3

Notes:

168

敗

Kun:

On:

Radical:

Meaning:

Stroke Order

Words that use [敗]:

Use [敗] in a sentence:

1

2

3

Notes:

169

散

Stroke Order

Kun:

On:

Radical:

Meaning:

Words that use [散]:

Use [散] in a sentence:

1

2

3

Notes:

170

数

Stroke Order

Kun:

On:

Radical:

Meaning:

Words that use [数]:

Use [数] in a sentence:

1

2

3

Notes:

171

断

Kun:

On:

Radical:

Meaning:

Stroke Order

Words that use [断]:

Use [断] in a sentence:

1

2

3

Notes:

172

易

Kun:

On:

Radical:

Meaning:

Stroke Order

Words that use [易]:

Use [易] in a sentence:

1

2

3

Notes:

173

昔

Stroke Order

Kun:

On:

Radical:

Meaning:

Words that use [昔]:

Use [昔] in a sentence:

1

2

3

Notes:

174

昨

Kun:

On:

Radical:

Meaning:

Stroke Order

Words that use [昨]:

Use [昨] in a sentence:

1

2

3

Notes:

175

晩

Kun:

On:

Radical:

Meaning:

Stroke Order

Words that use [晩]:

Use [晩] in a sentence:

1

2

3

Notes:

176

景

Kun:

On:

Radical:

Meaning:

Stroke Order

Words that use [景]:

Use [景] in a sentence:

1

2

3

Notes:

177

晴

Stroke Order

Kun:

On: Radical:

Meaning:

Words that use [晴]:

Use [晴] in a sentence:

1

2

3

Notes:

178

暗

Kun:

On:

Radical:

Meaning:

Stroke Order

Words that use [暗]:

Use [暗] in a sentence:

1

2

3

Notes:

暮

179

Stroke Order

Kun:

On: Radical:

Meaning:

Words that use [暮]:

Use [暮] in a sentence:

1

2

3

Notes:

180

曲

Kun:

On:

Radical:

Meaning:

Stroke Order

Words that use [曲]:

Use [曲] in a sentence:

1

2

3

Notes:

181

Kun:

On: Radical:

Meaning:

Stroke Order

Words that use [更]:

Use [更] in a sentence:

1

2

3

Notes:

182

最

Kun:

On:

Radical:

Meaning:

Stroke Order

Words that use [最]:

Use [最] in a sentence:

1

2

3

Notes:

183

望

Kun:

On:

Radical:

Meaning:

Stroke Order

Words that use [望]:

Use [望] in a sentence:

1

2

3

Notes:

184

期

Kun:

On:

Radical:

Meaning:

Stroke Order

Words that use [期]:

Use [期] in a sentence:

1

2

3

Notes:

185

未

Stroke Order

Kun:

On:

Radical:

Meaning:

Words that use [未]:

Use [未] in a sentence:

1

2

3

Notes:

186

末

Kun:

On:

Radical:

Meaning:

Stroke Order

Words that use [末]:

Use [末] in a sentence:

1

2

3

Notes:

187

東

Stroke Order

Kun:

On:

Radical:

Meaning:

Words that use [東]:

Use [東] in a sentence:

1

2

3

Notes:

188

杯

Kun:

On:

Radical:

Meaning:

Stroke Order

Words that use [杯]:

Use [杯] in a sentence:

1

2

3

Notes:

189

果

Stroke Order

Kun:

On: Radical:

Meaning:

Words that use [果]:

Use [果] in a sentence:

1

2

3

Notes:

190

格

Stroke Order

Kun:

On:

Radical:

Meaning:

Words that use [格]:

Use [格] in a sentence:

1

2

3

Notes:

191

構

Kun:

On:

Radical:

Meaning:

Stroke Order

Words that use [構]:

Use [構] in a sentence:

1

2

3

Notes:

192

様

Kun:

On:

Radical:

Meaning:

Stroke Order

Words that use [様]:

Use [様] in a sentence:

1

2

3

Notes:

193

権

Kun:

On:

Radical:

Meaning:

Stroke Order

Words that use [権]:

Use [権] in a sentence:

1

2

3

Notes:

194

横

Stroke Order

Kun:

On:

Radical:

Meaning:

Words that use [横]:

Use [横] in a sentence:

1

2

3

Notes:

195

機

Stroke Order

Kun:

On:

Radical:

Meaning:

Words that use [機]:

Use [機] in a sentence:

1

2

3

Notes:

196

欠

Stroke Order

Kun:

On:

Radical:

Meaning:

Words that use [欠]:

Use [欠] in a sentence:

1

2

3

Notes:

197

次

Kun:

On:

Radical:

Meaning:

Stroke Order

Words that use [次]:

Use [次] in a sentence:

1

2

3

Notes:

198

欲

Kun:

On:

Radical:

Meaning:

Stroke Order

Words that use [欲]:

Use [欲] in a sentence:

1

2

3

Notes:

199

歯

Kun:

On: Radical:

Meaning:

Stroke Order

Words that use [歯]:

Use [歯] in a sentence:

1

2

3

Notes:

200

歳

Kun:

On:

Radical:

Meaning:

Stroke Order

Words that use [歳]:

Use [歳] in a sentence:

1

2

3

Notes:

残

Stroke Order

201

残

Kun:

On:

Radical:

Meaning:

Words that use [残]:

Use [残] in a sentence:

1

2

3

Notes:

段

Stroke Order

202

段

Kun:

On:

Radical:

Meaning:

Words that use [段]:

Use [段] in a sentence:

1

2

3

Notes:

203

殺

Stroke Order

Kun:

On:

Radical:

Meaning:

Words that use [殺]:

Use [殺] in a sentence:

1

2

3

Notes:

204

民

Kun:

On:

Radical:

Meaning:

Stroke Order

Words that use [民]:

Use [民] in a sentence:

1

2

3

Notes:

205

求

Stroke Order

Kun:

On:

Radical:

Meaning:

Words that use [求]:

Use [求] in a sentence:

1

2

3

Notes:

決

Stroke Order

206

決

Kun:

On:

Radical:

Meaning:

Words that use [決]:

Use [決] in a sentence:

1

2

3

Notes:

207

治

Stroke Order

Kun:

On:

Radical:

Meaning:

Words that use [治]:

Use [治] in a sentence:

1

2

3

Notes:

208

法

法

Stroke Order

Kun:

On:

Radical:

Meaning:

Words that use [法]:

Use [法] in a sentence:

1

2

3

Notes:

209

泳

Kun:

On:

Radical:

Meaning:

Stroke Order

Words that use [泳]:

Use [泳] in a sentence:

1

2

3

Notes:

210

洗

Kun:

On:

Radical:

Meaning:

Stroke Order

Words that use [洗]:

Use [洗] in a sentence:

1

2

3

Notes:

211

活

Kun:

On:

Radical:

Meaning:

Stroke Order

Words that use [活]:

Use [活] in a sentence:

1

2

3

Notes:

212

流

Kun:

On:

Radical:

Meaning:

Stroke Order

Words that use [流]:

Use [流] in a sentence:

1

2

3

Notes:

213

浮

Stroke Order

Kun:

On:

Radical:

Meaning:

Words that use [浮]:

Use [浮] in a sentence:

1

2

3

Notes:

214

消

Kun:

On:

Radical:

Meaning:

Stroke Order

Words that use [消]:

Use [消] in a sentence:

1

2

3

Notes:

215

深

Kun:

On:

Radical:

Meaning:

Stroke Order

Words that use [深]:

Use [深] in a sentence:

1

2

3

Notes:

216

済

Kun:

On:　　　　　　　　　　　Radical:

Meaning:

Stroke Order

Words that use [済]:

Use [済] in a sentence:

1

2

3

Notes:

Stroke Order

217 渡

Kun:

On:

Radical:

Meaning:

Words that use [渡]:

Use [渡] in a sentence:

1

2

3

Notes:

218

港

Kun:

On:

Radical:

Meaning:

Stroke Order

Words that use [港]:

Use [港] in a sentence:

1

2

3

Notes:

219

満

Stroke Order

Kun:

On:

Radical:

Meaning:

Words that use [満]:

Use [満] in a sentence:

1

2

3

Notes:

220

演

Stroke Order

Kun:

On:

Radical:

Meaning:

Words that use [演]:

Use [演] in a sentence:

1

2

3

Notes:

Stroke Order

221

点

Kun:

On:

Radical:

Meaning:

Words that use [点]:

Use [点] in a sentence:

1

2

3

Notes:

222

然

Kun:

On:

Radical:

Meaning:

Stroke Order

Words that use [然]:

Use [然] in a sentence:

1

2

3

Notes:

223

煙

Kun:

On:

Radical:

Meaning:

Stroke Order

Words that use [煙]:

Use [煙] in a sentence:

1

2

3

Notes:

224

熱

Kun:

On:

Radical:

Meaning:

Stroke Order

Words that use [熱]:

Use [熱] in a sentence:

1

2

3

Notes:

225

犯

Kun:

On:

Radical:

Meaning:

Stroke Order

Words that use [犯]:

Use [犯] in a sentence:

1

2

3

Notes:

226

状

Stroke Order

Kun:

On:

Radical:

Meaning:

Words that use [状]:

Use [状] in a sentence:

1

2

3

Notes:

227

猫

Stroke Order

Kun:

On:

Radical:

Meaning:

Words that use [猫]:

Use [猫] in a sentence:

1

2

3

Notes:

228

王

Kun:

On:

Radical:

Meaning:

Stroke Order

Words that use [王]:

Use [王] in a sentence:

1

2

3

Notes:

現

Stroke Order

229

現

Kun:

On:

Radical:

Meaning:

Words that use [現]:

Use [現] in a sentence:

1

2

3

Notes:

球

Stroke Order

230

球

Kun:

On:

Radical:

Meaning:

Words that use [球]:

Use [球] in a sentence:

1

2

3

Notes:

Stroke Order

231

産

Kun:

On:

Radical:

Meaning:

Words that use [産]:

Use [産] in a sentence:

1

2

3

Notes:

232

由

Kun:

On:

Radical:

Meaning:

Stroke Order

Words that use [由]:

Use [由] in a sentence:

1

2

3

Notes:

233

Stroke Order

Kun:

On:

Radical:

Meaning:

Words that use [申]:

Use [申] in a sentence:

1

2

3

Notes:

234

留

Kun:

On:

Radical:

Meaning:

Stroke Order

Words that use [留]:

Use [留] in a sentence:

1

2

3

Notes:

235

番

Kun:

On:

Radical:

Meaning:

Stroke Order

Words that use [番]:

Use [番] in a sentence:

1

2

3

Notes:

236

疑

Kun:

On:

Radical:

Meaning:

Stroke Order

Words that use [疑]:

Use [疑] in a sentence:

1

2

3

Notes:

237

疲

Kun:

On:

Radical:

Meaning:

Stroke Order

Words that use [疲]:

Use [疲] in a sentence:

1

2

3

Notes:

238

痛

Kun:

On:

Radical:

Meaning:

Stroke Order

Words that use [痛]:

Use [痛] in a sentence:

1

2

3

Notes:

239

登

Stroke Order

Kun:

On:

Radical:

Meaning:

Words that use [登]:

Use [登] in a sentence:

1

2

3

Notes:

240

皆

Kun:

On:

Radical:

Meaning:

Stroke Order

Words that use [皆]:

Use [皆] in a sentence:

1

2

3

Notes:

241

盗

Kun:

On:

Radical:

Meaning:

Stroke Order

Words that use [盗]:

Use [盗] in a sentence:

1

2

3

Notes:

242

直

Stroke Order

Kun:

On:

Radical:

Meaning:

Words that use [直]:

Use [直] in a sentence:

1

2

3

Notes:

243

相

Stroke Order

Kun:

On:

Radical:

Meaning:

Words that use [相]:

Use [相] in a sentence:

1

2

3

Notes:

244

眠

Kun:

On:

Radical:

Meaning:

Stroke Order

Words that use [眠]:

Use [眠] in a sentence:

1

2

3

Notes:

Vocabulary & Reading Comprehension

SET 1

WORDS WITH N3 KANJI (VOLUME 1-2)		ADDITIONAL VOCABULARY	
愛(いと)しの	dear; beloved; darling	楽(たの)しい	enjoyable; fun; pleasant; happy; delightful
彼(かれ)	he; him; boyfriend	誰(だれ)	who
式(しき)	ceremony	使(つか)う	to use (a thing, method, etc.); to make use of; to put to use
想像(そうぞう)	imagination; guess	挨拶(あいさつ)	greeting; greetings; salutation; salute; polite set phrase used when meeting or parting from somebody
場所(ばしょ)	place; location; spot; position; room; space	お願(ねが)い	request; favour (to ask); wish
招待(しょうたい)	invitation	何(なに)	what
曲(きょく)	composition; piece of music; song; track (on a record)	難(むずか)しい	difficult; hard; troublesome; complicated; serious (disease, problem, etc.)
役割(やくわり)	part; assigning (allotment of) parts; role; duties	家(いえ)	house; residence; dwelling
引(ひ)き出物(でもの)	gift; souvenir	考(かんが)える	to think (about, of); to think over; to ponder; to contemplate; to reflect (on); to meditate (on)
非常(ひじょう)	emergency	今日(きょう)	today; this day
判断(はんだん)	judgment; judgement; decision; conclusion; adjudication	前(まえ)	in front (of); before (e.g. the house); ago; before; previously; prior
昨日(きのう)	yesterday	見(み)に行(い)く	to go to see (something, someone); to visit
晴(は)れる	to clear up; to clear away; to be sunny; to stop raining		
日(ひ)が暮(く)れる	to set (sun); to become dark		
支度(したく)	preparation; arrangements		
散歩(さんぽ)	walk; stroll		
探(さが)しに	in search of; in order to look for		
数力所(すうかしょ)	various places; several sources		
最高(さいこう)	most; highest; maximum; uppermost; supreme; best; wonderful; finest		
結婚(けっこん)	marriage		
決(き)める	to decide; to choose; to determine; to make up one's mind; to resolve; to set one's heart on		
実際(じっさい)	practicality; practical; reality; actuality; actual conditions		

SET 1

NEW KANJI AND VOCABULARY

NOTES

SET 1

VOCABULARY					FURIGANA	MEANING	NOTES
	し	に				in search of; in order to look for	
	度					preparation; arrangements	
	像					imagination; guess	
	れ	る				to clear up; to clear away; to be sunny; to stop raining	
場						place; location; spot; position; room; space	
	待					invitation	
	日					yesterday	
						part; assigning (allotment of) parts; role; duties	
	き	出	物			gift; souvenir	
						emergency	
						judgment; judgement; decision; conclusion; adjudication	
	力					various places; several sources	
						ceremony	
日	が		れ	る		to set (sun); to become dark	
						composition; piece of music; song; track (on a record)	
	歩					walk; stroll	
						he; him; boyfriend	
	し	の				dear; beloved; darling	

SET 1

VOCABULARY				FURIGANA	MEANING	NOTES
	際				practicality; practical; reality; actuality; actual conditions	
	め	る			to decide; to choose; to make up one's mind; to resolve	
結					marriage	
	高				most; highest; maximum; supreme; best; wonderful; finest	

SET 1 READING COMPREHENSION

愛しの彼とついに結婚することになった。

どんな式にしようかなと想像するととても楽しいけど、場所はどこにするか、誰を招待するか、

どんな曲を使うか、また誰にスピーチや挨拶の役割をお願いすべきか、引き出物は何にする

かなどを決めるのは非常に判断が難しい。

昨日からずっと家で考えてるけど、決められないし、せっかく今日は晴れてるから、日が暮れる

前にぱっぱと支度して、散歩がてらアイディアを探しに数カ所実際に見に行こう。

最高のものにするぞ!

TRANSLATION

_____

_____

_____

_____

_____

_____

_____

SET 1

TRANSLATION

NEW KANJI AND VOCABULARY

NOTES

SET 1

WITH FURIGANA

愛しの彼とついに結婚することになった。

どんな式にしようかなと想像するととても楽しいけど、場所はどこにするか、

誰を招待するか、どんな曲を使うか、また誰にスピーチや挨拶の役割を

お願いすべきか、引き出物は何にするかなどを決めるのは非常に判断が

難しい。

昨日からずっと家で考えてるけど、決められないし、せっかく今日は晴れてる

から、日が暮れる前にぱっぱと支度して、散歩がてらアイディアを探しに

数カ所実際に見に行こう。

最高のものにするぞ!

NEW KANJI AND VOCABULARY

NOTES

SET 2

WORDS WITH N3 (VOLUME 1-2)

感謝(かんしゃ)	thanks; gratitude	怒(おこ)る	to get angry; to get mad
最後(さいご)	end; conclusion	愛想(あいそ)	amiability; friendliness; affability; sociability; fondness (of someone); affection; liking
昔(むかし)	olden days; former	恐怖(きょうふ)	fear; dread; dismay; terror; horror; scare; panic
必死(ひっし)	frantic; frenetic; desperate	今更(いまさら)	now (when it is already much too late); at this stage
忙(いそが)しい	busy; occupied; hectic; restless; hurried; fidgety	見放(みはな)す	to abandon; to give up on; to desert
形(かたち)	form; shape; figure	望(のぞ)み	wish; desire; hope
得(え)る	to get; to earn; to acquire; to procure; to gain; to secure; to attain; to obtain; to win	念(ねん)の為(ため)	(just) making sure; just to be sure; just in case; for caution's sake
無形(むけい)	abstract; immaterial; moral; spiritual; intangible	結果(けっか)	result; consequence; outcome; effect; to spend (time); to live one's life
忘(わす)れる	to forget; to leave carelessly; to be forgetful of; to forget about; to forget (an article)	夫(おっと)	husband
恥(は)ずべき	disgraceful; shameful	変(か)える	to change; to alter; to transform; to convert; to turn; to vary; to reform; to revise; to amend
性格(せいかく)	character (of a person); personality; disposition; nature	居(い)る	to be (of animate objects); to exist; to stay

ADDITIONAL VOCABULARY

嫁(よめ)	wife; bride	10年(じゅうねん)	10 years
今(いま)	now; the present time; just now; soon; immediately	以上(いじょう)	not less than; ... and more; ... and upwards
気持(きも)ち	feeling; sensation; mood; state of mind; thought; sentiment; consideration; solicitude; gratitude	前(まえ)	the last (i.e. immediately preceding) (e.g. "the last mayor"); previous; one-time; former; before; earlier
込(こ)める	to put into (e.g. emotion, effort); to load (a gun, etc.); to charge	仕事(しごと)	work; job; labor; labour; business; task; assignment; occupation; employment
一緒(いっしょ)に	together (with); at the same time; in a lump	毎日(まいにち)	every day
旅行(りょこう)	travel; trip; journey; excursion; tour	送(おく)る	to send (a thing); to dispatch; to despatch; to transmit
行(い)く	to go; to move (in a direction or towards a specific location)	お金(かね)	money
旅行(りょこう)	travel; trip; journey; excursion; tour	思(おも)い出(で)	memories; recollections; reminiscence
事(こと)	thing; matter	記憶(きおく)	memory; recollection; remembrance

SET 2 VOCABULARY

ADDITIONAL VOCABULARY

何(なに)もない	there is nothing	逆(ぎゃく)に	conversely; on the contrary
気(き)がつく	to notice; to become aware; to perceive; to realize; to realise	感(かん)じる	to feel; to sense; to experience
誕生(たんじょうび)	birthday	過(す)ぎた事(こと)	bygones; the past; past event
穏(おだ)やか	calm; quiet; gentle; peaceful; mild	私(わたし)	I; me
尽(つ)かす	to use completely; to use up; to exhaust	一番(いちばん)	number one; first; first place; best; most
思(おも)う	to think; to consider; to believe; to reckon		

NEW KANJI AND VOCABULARY

NOTES

SET 2

VOCABULARY				FURIGANA	MEANING	NOTES
	み				now (when it is already much too late); at this stage	
見	す				to abandon; to give up on; to desert	
					olden days; former	
今					now (when it is already much too late); at this stage	
	後				end; conclusion	
					form; shape; figure	
	る				to get; to earn; to acquire; to gain; to secure; to attain	
無					abstract; immaterial; moral; spiritual; intangible	
	る				to get angry; to get mad	
	ず	べ	き		disgraceful; shameful	
					character (of a person); personality; disposition; nature	
	の	為			(just) making sure; just in case; for caution's sake	
	れ	る			to forget; to leave carelessly; to be forgetful of	
					fear; dread; dismay; terror; horror; scare; panic	
	し	い			busy; occupied; hectic; restless; hurried; fidgety	
	死				frantic; frenetic; desperate	
					amiability; friendliness; affability; sociability; affection; liking	
	謝				thanks; gratitude	

SET 2

VOCABULARY				FURIGANA	MEANING	NOTES
結					result; consequence; outcome; effect; to spend (time)	
					husband	
	える	る			to change; to alter; to transform; to reform; to revise; to amend	
	る				to be (of animate objects); to exist; to stay	

SET 2

嫁に今までの感謝の気持ちを込めて、一緒に旅行に行くことにした。

最後に旅行したのは昔の事で10年以上前になる。

この10年、仕事を必死にこなし忙しい毎日を送ってきた結果、形のあるお金は得たけど、無形である嫁との思い出や記憶は何もない事に気がついた。

嫁の誕生日すら忘れてしまうなんて、夫として恥ずべき事だ。穏やかな性格の嫁は怒らないが、愛想を尽かされたのかと思うと逆に恐怖に感じた。

過ぎた事は今更変える事はできないけど、今も見放さずに居てくれてる嫁とずっと一緒にいることが私の一番の望みだ。

念の為、スマホのリマインダーに嫁の誕生日をセットした。

TRANSLATION

SET 2

TRANSLATION

NEW KANJI AND VOCABULARY

NOTES

SET 2

WITH FURIGANA

嫁に今までの感謝の気持ちを込めて、一緒に旅行に行くことにした。

最後に旅行したのは昔の事で10年以上前になる。

この10年、仕事を必死にこなし忙しい毎日を送ってきた結果、形のあるお金は

得たけど、無形である嫁との思い出や記憶は何もない事に気がついた。

嫁の誕生日すら忘れてしまうなんて、夫として恥ずべき事だ。穏やかな性格の

嫁は怒らないが、愛想を尽かされたのかと思うと逆に恐怖に感じた。

過ぎた事は今更変える事はできないけど、今も見放さずに居てくれてる嫁と

ずっと一緒にいることが私の一番の望みだ。

念の為、スマホのリマインダーに嫁の誕生日をセットした。

NEW KANJI AND VOCABULARY

NOTES

SET 3 — VOCABULARY

WORDS WITH N3 KANJI (VOLUME 1-2)

格闘技(かくとうぎ)	martial arts which involve fighting without weapons; combat sport; one-on-one fighting sport	折(お)る	to break; to fracture; to break off; to snap off; to pick (e.g. flowers); to fold; to bend
最 (もっと)も	most; extremely	場慣(ばな)れ	experience; being accustomed (to something); poise in a critical situation
採用(さいよう)	use; adoption; acceptance	足払(あしばら)い	foot sweep; sweeping one's opponent's legs from under them (judo, etc.)
才能(さいのう)	talent; ability	組(く)み合(あ)わせる	to join together; to combine; to join up
易(やす)い	easy	守(まも)る	to protect; to guard; to defend; to keep (i.e. a promise); to abide (by the rules); to observe; to obey; to follow
打撃(だげき)	blow; shock; strike; damage	無残(むざん)	cruel; merciless; atrocious; ruthless; cold-blooded; pitiful; tragic; horrible; miserable
投(な)げ技(わざ)	throw or throwing technique (sumo, judo)	悲(かな)しい	sad; miserable; unhappy; sorrowful; lamentable; deplorable; grievous
実戦(じっせん)	combat; battle; action; active service; actual fighting	相手(あいて)	companion; partner; company; opponent (sports, etc.)
成人(せいじん)	adult (esp. person 20 years old or over); grownup; becoming an adult; coming of age; growing up (to be a man, woman)	状態(じょうたい)	state; condition; situation; appearance; circumstances
最低限(さいていげん)	minimum; at the very least	一番(いちばん)	number one; first; first place; best; most
敗(やぶ)れる	to be defeated; to be beaten; to be unsuccessful; to lose	理由(りゆう)	reason; pretext; motive
抱(いだ)く	to hold in one's arms (e.g. a baby); to embrace; to hug; to have (a thought or feeling); to harbor (suspicion, doubt, etc.)		

ADDITIONAL VOCABULARY

種類(しゅるい)	variety; kind; type; category	意識(いしき)	consciousness; becoming aware (of); awareness; sense
今(いま)	now; the present time; just now; soon; immediately	特徴(とくちょう)	feature; trait; characteristic; peculiarity; distinction
興味(きょうみ)	interest (in something); curiosity (about something); zest (for)	男(おとこ)	man; male
軍隊(ぐんたい)	armed forces; military; troops	大切(たいせつ)な人(ひと)	special someone; special person; precious one; significant other
個人(こじん)	individual; private person; personal; private	目(め)の前(まえ)	before one's eyes; in front of one; under one's nose
頼(たよ)る	to rely on; to depend on; to count on; to turn to (for help)	思(おも)い	thought; imagination; mind; heart; feelings; emotion; sentiment; experience

SET 3

VOCABULARY

ADDITIONAL VOCABULARY

無(な)い	not; nonexistent; not being (there)	事(こと)	thing; matter
幅広(はばひろ)い	extensive; wide; broad	嫌(いや)	disagreeable; detestable; unpleasant; reluctant
層(そう)	class; stratum; bracket; group	別(べつ)に	(not) particularly; (not) especially; (not) specially; separately; apart; additionally; extra
人(ひと)	man; person	骨(ほね)	bone
習(なら)い	as is habit; the way life normally is		

NEW KANJI AND VOCABULARY

NOTES

SET 3

NEW KANJI AND VOCABULARY

NOTES

SET 3

VOCABULARY			FURIGANA	MEANING	NOTES
	る			to protect; to defend; to keep(i.e. a promise); to follow (i.e. rules)	
場	れ			experience; being accustomed (to something)	
	れ	る		to be defeated; to be beaten; to be unsuccessful; to lose	
	れ	人		adult (esp. person 20 years old or over); grownup; coming of age	
無				cruel; merciless; atrocious; ruthless; cold-blooded; miserable	
	撃			blow; shock; strike; damage	
	げ			throw or throwing technique (sumo, judo)	
				combat; battle; action; active service; actual fighting	
	い			easy	
	低	限		minimum; at the very least	
	能			talent; ability	
	く			to hold in one's arms (e.g. a baby); to hug	
	る			to break; to fracture; to break off; to snap off; to pick (e.g. flowers)	
	用			use; adoption; acceptance	
足	い			foot sweep; sweeping one's opponent's legs (judo, etc.)	
組み		わせる		to join together; to combine; to join up	
	も			most; extremely	
格	闘			martial arts (without weapons); combat sport; 1-on-1 fight sport	

SET 3 — VOCABULARY EXERCISE

VOCABULARY					FURIGANA	MEANING	NOTES
一						number one; first; first place; best; most	
	し	い				sad; miserable; sorrowful; lamentable; deplorable; grievous	
	態					state; condition; situation; appearance; circumstances	
理						reason; pretext; motive	
	手					companion; partner; company; opponent (sports, etc.)	

SET 3

格闘技にはいろんな種類があるが、今最も興味があるのがクラヴマガです。

クラブマガはイスラエルの軍隊も採用しているのもあり、個人の才能に頼ること無く、

幅広い層の人が習い易く、打撃、足払い、投げ技などを組み合わせた実戦を

意識しているのが特徴だ。

成人の男として最低限、大切な人を守れるようになりたいし、目の前で無残にも敗れて

悲しい思いを抱く事になるのは嫌だってのもある。

でも、別に相手をボコボコにして骨を折ってやるとかではなく、相手にビビらないくらい

の場慣れしている状態になりたいのが一番の理由かな。

TRANSLATION

SET 3

TRANSLATION

NEW KANJI AND VOCABULARY

NOTES

SET 3

WITH FURIGANA

格闘技にはいろんな種類があるが、今最も興味があるのがクラヴマガです。

クラブマガはイスラエルの軍隊も採用しているのもあり、個人の才能に頼る

こと無く、幅広い層の人が習い易く、打撃、足払い、投げ技などを組み合わせた

実戦を意識しているのが特徴だ。

成人の男として最低限、大切な人を守れるようになりたいし、目の前で無残

にも敗れて悲しい思いを抱く事になるのは嫌だってのもある。

でも、別に相手をボコボコにして骨を折ってやるとかではなく、相手に

ビビらないくらいの場慣れしている状態になりたいのが一番の理由かな。

NEW KANJI AND VOCABULARY

NOTES

SET 4 — VOCABULARY

WORDS WITH N3 KANJI (VOLUME 1-2)

天才(てんさい)	genius; prodigy; natural gift	放送(ほうそう)	broadcast; broadcasting
非常(ひじょう)に	very; extremely; exceedingly	押(お)し付(つ)け	imposition (i.e. of rules, of a decision); compulsion
暮(く)らす	to live; to get along; to spend (time)	合格(ごうかく)	success; passing (e.g. exam); eligibility
所謂(いわゆる)	what is called; as it is called; the so-called; so to speak	国内(こくない)	internal; domestic
景色(けしき)	scenery; scene; landscape	受(う)ける	to receive; to get; to undergo (e.g. surgery); to take (a test); to accept (a challenge)
当(あ)たり前(まえ)	natural; reasonable; obvious	全(まった)く	really; truly; entirely; completely; wholly; perfectly; indeed
掛(か)ける	to spend (time, money); to expend; to use; to hang up (e.g. a coat, a picture on the wall); to let hang; to suspend (from); to hoist (e.g. sail); to raise (e.g. flag)	上級国民(じょうきゅうこくみん)	the elite (class)
指折(ゆびお)り	leading; prominent; eminent; foremost; distinguished	視座(しざ)	vantage point; viewpoint; standpoint; outlook
生徒(せいと)	pupil; student; schoolchild	都内(とない)	(within) the (Tokyo) metropolitan area
親御(おやご)さん	another's parent; another's parents	高級住宅街(こうきゅうじゅうたくがい)	high-end residential area; affluent neighbourhood
政治家(せいじか)	politician; statesman	情報(じょうほう)	information; news; intelligence; advices
暗(くら)い	dark; gloomy; murky; depressed; dispirited; down in the dumps; dark (mood)	傾向(けいこう)	tendency; trend; inclination
怖(こわ)い	scary; frightening; eerie; dreadful	実際(じっさい)に	virtually; practically; in practice; actually; currently; presently
息子(むすこ)さん	son [Honorific or respectful]		

ADDITIONAL VOCABULARY

以外(いがい)	with the exception of; excepting	高(たか)い	high; tall; high (level); above average (in degree, quality, etc.)
入学(にゅうがく)	entry to school or university; matriculation; enrolment (in university, etc.) (enrollment)	見(み)る	to see; to look; to watch; to view; to observe
難(むずか)しい	difficult; hard; troublesome; complicated; serious (disease, problem, etc.)	違(ちが)う	to differ (from); to vary
東大(とうだい)	University of Tokyo	教育(きょういく)	education; schooling; training; instruction; teaching; upbringing
為(ため)に	for; for the sake of; to one's advantage; in favor of; in favour of; on behalf of	お金(かね)	money

SET 4

ADDITIONAL VOCABULARY

塾(じゅく)	cram school; private tutoring school	住(す)む	to live (of humans); to reside; to inhabit; to dwell; to abide
通(かよ)い始(はじ)める	to begin to attend (e.g. school)	有名(ゆうめい)	famous
大(おお)きく	in a big way; on a grand scale	話(はな)す	to talk; to speak; to converse; to chat; to tell; to explain; to narrate; to mention; to describe; to discuss
今(いま)	now; the present time; just now; soon; immediately	姿(すがた)	figure; form; shape; appearance; dress; guise; state; condition; picture; image
来(き)る	to come (spatially or temporally); to approach; to arrive	意外(いがい)	unexpected; surprising
環境(かんきょう)	environment; circumstance	普通(ふつう)	normal; ordinary; regular; usual; common; average
人達(ひとたち)	people	強(つよ)い	strong; potent; competent; domineering; tough
種類(しゅるい)	variety; kind; type; category	自分(じぶん)	myself; yourself; oneself; himself; herself; I; me
違(ちが)う	to differ (from); to vary; to not match the correct (answer, etc.)	体験(たいけん)	(practical) experience; personal experience; hands-on experience; first-hand experience
沢山(たくさん)	a lot; lots; plenty; many; a large number; much; a great deal; a good deal	大切(たいせつ)	important; necessary; indispensable; beloved; precious; dear; cherished; valuable
と言(い)われる	to be called ...; to be referred to as ...	思(おも)う	to think; to consider; to believe; to reckon
人達(ひとたち)	people		

NEW KANJI AND VOCABULARY

NOTES

SET 4

NEW KANJI AND VOCABULARY

NOTES

SET 4

VOCABULARY				FURIGANA	MEANING	NOTES
					success; passing (e.g. exam); eligibility	
	送				broadcast; broadcasting	
	ら	す			to live; to get along; to spend (time)	
	謂				what is called; as it is called; the so-called; so to speak	
	色				scenery; scene; landscape	
	い				scary; frightening; eerie; dreadful	
生					pupil; student; schoolchild	
					leading; prominent; eminent; foremost; distinguished	
親		さ	ん		another's parent; another's parents	
	子	さ	ん		son [Honorific or respectful]	
		家			politician; statesman	
	い				dark; gloomy; murky; depressed; dispirited; dark (mood)	
	け	る			to spend (time, money); to expend; to hang up (e.g. coat etc.)	
国					internal; domestic	
	た	り	前		natural; reasonable; obvious	
	し		け		imposition (i.e. of rules, of a decision); compulsion	
		に			very; extremely; exceedingly	
天					genius; prodigy; natural gift	

SET 4

VOCABULARY					FURIGANA	MEANING	NOTES
都						(within) the (Tokyo) metropolitan area	
	く					really; truly; entirely; completely; wholly; perfectly; indeed	
	際	に				virtually; practically; in practice; actually; currently; presently	
視						vantage point; viewpoint; standpoint; outlook	
上	級	国				the elite (class)	
高	級	住		街		high-end residential area; affluent neighbourhood	
						information; news; intelligence; advices	
傾						tendency; trend; inclination	
	け	る				to receive; to get; to undergo (e.g. surgery); to take (a test)	

SET 4

天才以外は入学は非常に難しい東大。

そこに合格する為に塾に通い始めたが、国内なのにカルチャーショックを大きく受けている。

今まで暮らして来た環境の人達とは種類が全く違うタイプが沢山いるからだ。

所謂『上級国民』と言われる人達。視座が高く見ている景色が違う。

当たり前のように教育にお金を掛けているし、都内でも指折りの高級住宅街に住んでいる。

生徒の親御さんには有名な政治家もいて、テレビでは暗くて怖いイメージだけど、息子さんと話している姿は意外と普通だった。

やっぱりテレビが放送する情報はイメージの押し付けが強い傾向があるから、実際に自分が体験することが大切だなと思った。

TRANSLATION

SET 4

TRANSLATION

NEW KANJI AND VOCABULARY

NOTES

SET 4

WITH FURIGANA

天才以外は入学は非常に難しい東大。

そこに合格する為に塾に通い始めたが、国内なのにカルチャーショックを

大きく受けている。

今まで暮らして来た環境の人達とは種類が全く違うタイプが沢山いるからだ。

所謂『上級国民』と言われる人達。視座が高く見ている景色が違う。

当たり前のように教育にお金を掛けているし、都内でも指折りの高級住宅街

に住んでいる。

生徒の親御さんには有名な政治家もいて、テレビでは暗くて怖いイメージだ

けど、息子さんと話している姿は意外と普通だった。

やっぱりテレビが放送する情報はイメージの押し付けが強い傾向がある

から、実際に自分が体験することが大切だなと思った。

NEW KANJI AND VOCABULARY

NOTES

SET 5 — VOCABULARY

WORDS WITH N3 KANJI (VOLUME 1-2)

野球 (やきゅう)	baseball	次 (つぎ)	next; following; subsequent
不格好 (ぶかっこう)	unshapely; ill-formed; misshapen	皆 (みんな)	everyone; everybody; all; everything
あり様 (さま)	state; condition; circumstances; sight; spectacle;	満足 (まんぞく)	satisfaction; contentment; gratification
申 (もう) し込 (こ) む	to apply for; to make an application; to propose (marriage); to offer (mediation)	参加 (さんか)	participation; joining; entry; adherence
番 (ばん)	number (in a series); rank; standing; position; (one's) turn	放課後 (ほうかご)	after school (at the end of the day)
活躍 (かつやく)	activity (esp. energetic); great efforts; conspicuous service	部活動 (ぶかつどう)	club activities; extracurricular activities
決勝戦 (けっしょうせん)	championship game; finals (of a tournament); deciding round	所属 (しょぞく)	belonging to (a group, organization, etc.); affiliation (with); being attached to; being under the control of
相手 (あいて)	companion; partner; company; other party; addressee	最後 (さいご)	end; conclusion
点 (てん)	dot; spot; point; speck; mark; point (in a game); score; goal; run	優勝 (ゆうしょう)	overall victory; championship
残 (のこ) る	to remain; to be left	上位 (じょうい)	superior (in rank); top; ranking
盗塁 (とうるい)	base stealing; steal; stolen base	最善 (さいぜん)	the very best; utmost
欲 (よく)	greed; craving; desire; appetite; hunger; avarice; wants		

ADDITIONAL VOCABULARY

私 (わたし)	I; me	対 (たい)	to (e.g. "winning a game five to three"); opposite; opposition; versus; vs.
進 (すす) む	to advance; to go forward; to precede; to go ahead (of)	負 (ま) ける	to lose; to be defeated
入 (い) れる	to put in; to let in; to take in; to bring in; to insert; to install (e.g. software); to set (a jewel, etc.); to ink in (e.g. tattoo)	良 (よ) い	good; excellent; fine; nice; pleasant; agreeable
小学生 (しょうがくせい)	elementary school student; primary school student; grade school student	思 (おも) い出 (で)	memories; recollections; reminiscence
中学生 (ちゅうがくせい)	junior high school student; middle school pupil	頭 (あたま)	head
行 (おこな) う	to perform; to do; to conduct oneself; to carry out	当時 (とうじ)	at that time; in those days
始 (はじ) める	to start; to begin; to commence; to initiate; to originate	足 (あし)	foot; paw; arm (of an octopus, squid, etc.); leg
頃 (ころ)	(approximate) time; around; about; toward	速 (はや) く	early; soon; quickly; swiftly; rapidly; fast

SET 5

ADDITIONAL VOCABULARY

思（おも）う	to think; to consider; to believe; to reckon	出塁（しゅつるい）	getting on base; reaching first base
毎日（まいにち）	every day	出来（でき）る	to be able (in a position) to do; to be up to the task
練習（れんしゅう）	practice; training; drill; (an) exercise; workout	言（い）えば	speaking of
試合（しあい）	match; game; bout; contest	出場（しゅつじょう）	(stage) appearance; performance; participation (e.g. in a tournament)
積極的（せっきょくてき）	positive; assertive; active; proactive; aggressive	一丸（いちがん）となって	in unison; as one; united [expression]
経験（けいけん）	experience	尽（づ）くし	all sorts of; all kinds of [suffix]
積（つ）む	to pile up; to stack	悔（くや）しい	vexing; annoying; frustrating; regrettable; mortifying
時（とき）	time; hour; moment	思（おも）い	thought; imagination; mind; heart; feelings; emotion; sentiment
行（おこな）われる	to be done; to be practiced; to be practised; to take place; to be held; to be prevalent; to be in fashion	今（いま）	now; the present time; just now; soon; immediately
大会（たいかい）	tournament; competition; mass meeting; convention; conference; gathering	十分（じゅうぶん）	enough; sufficient; plenty; adequate; satisfactory
結局（けっきょく）	after all; in the end; ultimately; eventually; conclusion; end		

NEW KANJI AND VOCABULARY

NOTES

SET 5

NEW KANJI AND VOCABULARY

NOTES

SET 5

VOCABULARY				FURIGANA	MEANING	NOTES
					participation; joining; entry; adherence	
不		好			unshapely; ill-formed; misshapen	
					everyone; everybody; all; everything	
	手				companion; partner; company; other party; addressee	
	塁				base stealing; steal; stolen base	
	躍				activity (esp. energetic); great efforts; conspicuous service	
					championship game; finals (of a tournament); deciding round	
あ	り				state; condition; circumstances; sight; spectacle;	
					dot; spot; point; speck; mark; point (in a game); score; goal; run	
	る				to remain; to be left	
					greed; craving; desire; appetite; hunger; avarice; wants	
	し	込	む		to apply for; to make an application; to propose(marriage)	
					next; following; subsequent	
部		動			club activities; extracurricular activities	
	足				satisfaction; contentment; gratification	
					number (in a series); rank; standing; position; (one's) turn	
	課	後			after school (at the end of the day)	
野					baseball	

SET 5

VOCABULARY				FURIGANA	MEANING	NOTES
	属				belonging to (a group, organization, etc.); affiliation	
	後				end; conclusion	
	勝				overall victory; championship	
上					superior (in rank); top; ranking	
	善				the very best; utmost	

SET 5

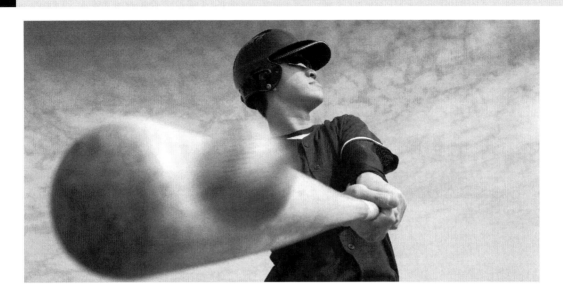

私は、小学生から中学生まで野球を行っていた。始めた頃は、不格好なあり様だったと思うが、毎日練習したものだ。申し込める試合には積極的に参加し、経験を積んだ。中学生の時は、放課後、行われる部活動に所属し、1番、サードで活躍したものだった。中学生最後の大会では、決勝戦まで進んだのだが、相手のチームから4点も入れられ、結局4対1で負けてしまったが、良い思い出として頭に残っている。当時の私は足も速く、出塁すると、盗塁も行うことが出来た。欲を言えば、優勝し次の上位大会に出場したかったが、皆チーム一丸となって最善を尽くし、負けて悔しい思いをしたが、今では十分満足している。

TRANSLATION

SET 5

TRANSLATION

NEW KANJI AND VOCABULARY

NOTES

SET 5

WITH FURIGANA

私は、小学生から中学生まで野球を行っていた。始めた頃は、不格好なあり様だったと思うが、毎日練習したものだ。申し込める試合には積極的に参加し、経験を積んだ。中学生の時は、放課後、行われる部活動に所属し、1番、サードで活躍したものだった。

中学生最後の大会では、決勝戦まで進んだのだが、相手のチームから4点も入れられ、結局4対1で負けてしまったが、良い思い出として頭に残っている。当時の私は足も速く、出塁すると、盗塁も行うことが出来た。欲を言えば、優勝し次の上位大会に出場したかったが、皆チーム一丸となって最善を尽くし、負けて悔しい思いをしたが、今では十分満足している。

NEW KANJI AND VOCABULARY

NOTES

SET 6 VOCABULARY

WORDS WITH N3 KANJI (VOLUME 1-2)

歯 (は)	tooth	未 (ま)だ	still; as yet; only
異状 (いじょう)	something wrong; accident; change; abnormality; aberration	治療 (ちりょう)	(medical) treatment; care; therapy; cure; remedy
欠 (か)ける	to be chipped; to be damaged; to be broken	済 (ず)み	arranged; taken care of; settled; completed; finished
歳 (とし)	year; age; years; past one's prime; old age	一杯 (いっぱい)	amount necessary to fill a container (e.g. cupful, spoonful, etc.); drink (usu. alcoholic)
痛 (いた)み	pain; ache; soreness; grief; distress	疲 (つか)れる	to get tired; to tire; to get fatigued; to become exhausted; to grow weary
眠 (ねむ)る	to sleep	自然 (しぜん)	nature
洗 (あら)い	washing	治 (なお)る	to get better; to get well; to recover (from an illness); to be cured; to be restored; to heal
直 (す)ぐにでも	right away; without delay; as soon as possible; very soon	横 (よこ)	horizontal (as opposed to vertical); lying down; beside; aside; next to
歯医者 (はいしゃ)	dentist	昨日 (きのう)	yesterday
一番 (いちばん)	number one; first; first place	感 (かん)じる	to feel; to sense; to experience
結果 (けっか)	result; consequence; outcome; effect; coming to fruition; bearing fruit	次第 (しだい)に	gradually (progress into a state); in sequence; in order; in turn
数段 (すうだん)	several (levels, floors)	必要 (ひつよう)	necessary; needed; essential; indispensable

ADDITIONAL VOCABULARY

昨日 (きのう)	yesterday	気持 (きもち)	feeling; sensation; mood; state of mind
夕食 (ゆうしょく)	evening meal; dinner	午前中 (ごぜんちゅう)	in the morning; during the morning
中 (ちゅう)	during (a certain time when one did or is doing something); under (construction, etc.); while	行 (い)き	the way there; outbound leg; outbound trip; departing leg
固 (かた)い	hard; solid; tough	良 (よ)く	nicely; properly; well; skillfully; skilfully
物 (もの)	thing; object; article; stuff; substance	来週 (らいしゅう)	next week
食 (た)べる	to eat	来 (く)る	to come (spatially or temporally); to approach; to arrive
時 (とき)	time; hour; moment	言 (い)う	to say; to utter; to declare
何 (なん)と	what; how; what (a) ...!; how ...!(indicates surprise, admiration etc.)	控 (ひか)える	to be temperate in; to refrain; to abstain; to hold back; to restrain oneself from excessive
一部 (いちぶ)	one part; one portion; one section; some	今日 (きょう)	today; this day
出 (で)る	to leave; to exit; to go out; to come out; to get out	思 (おも)う	to think; to consider; to believe; to reckon
夜 (よる)	evening; night	通院 (つういん)	going to the hospital for regular treatment
朝 (あさ)	morning	致 (いた)し方 (かた)ない	there's no (other) way; cannot be helped; unavoidable; inevitable; (there's) nothing one can do; having no choice

SET 6

ADDITIONAL VOCABULARY

起(お)きる	to get up; to rise; to blaze up (fire); to wake up; to be awake; to stay awake; to occur (usu. of unfavourable incidents); to happen; to take place	早(はや)く	early; soon
顔(かお)	face; visage; look; expression; countenance	休(やす)む	to be absent; to take a day off; to rest; to have a break
駆(か)け込(こ)む	to run into; to rush into; to (run and) seek refuge in; to take shelter in		

NEW KANJI AND VOCABULARY

NOTES

SET 6

VOCABULARY					FURIGANA	MEANING	NOTES
	れ	る				to get tired; to get fatigued; to become exhausted	
	み					arranged; taken care of; settled; completed; finished	
	医	者				dentist	
						year; age; years; past one's prime; old age	
	み					pain; ache; soreness; grief; distress	
自						nature	
	い					washing	
	ぐ	に	で	も		right away; without delay; as soon as possible; very soon	
	る					to sleep	
一						number one; first; first place	
結						result; consequence; outcome; effect; coming to fruition	
						several (levels, floors)	
	だ					still; as yet; only	
	療					(medical) treatment; care; therapy; cure; remedy	
	け	る				to be chipped; to be damaged; to be broken	
一						drink (usu. alcoholic)	
異						something wrong; accident; change; abnormality; aberration	
						tooth	

SET 6

VOCABULARY				FURIGANA	MEANING	NOTES
第	に				gradually (progress into a state); in sequence; in order; in turn	
要					necessary; needed; essential; indispensable	
日					yesterday	
じ	る				to feel; to sense; to experience	
					horizontal (as opposed to vertical); lying down; beside	
る					to get better; to get well; to recover (from an illness)	

SET 6

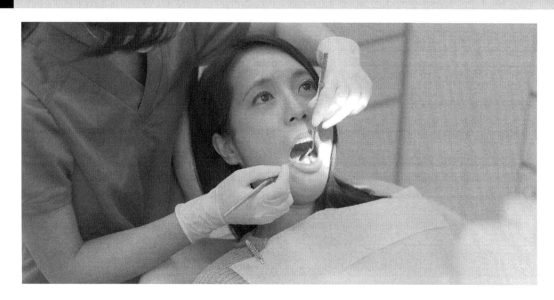

昨日、夕食中に固い物を食べた時に、歯の異状を感じた。何と歯が一部欠けて出てきた。

歳だなあと感じたが、次第に痛みも出てきて、その夜は、痛みでよく眠れないほどだった。

朝、起きて顔を洗い、直ぐにでも歯医者に駆け込みたい気持だった。午前中一番で

歯医者に行き、治療をしてもらった。その結果、数段良くなったが、未だ、治療が必要な

歯もあるので、来週も来るように言われた。治療済みになるまではしばらくかかるらしい。

アルコールは控えるように言われたので、今日は一杯のビールも控えようと思う。通院する

だけでも疲れるが、自然と治るはずはないので致し方ない。

今日は早く横になって休むつもりだ。

TRANSLATION

SET 6

TRANSLATION

NEW KANJI AND VOCABULARY

NOTES

SET 6

WITH FURIGANA

昨日、夕食中に固い物を食べた時に、歯の異状を感じた。何と歯が一部欠けて出てきた。歳だなあと感じたが、次第に痛みも出てきて、その夜は、痛みでよく眠れないほどだった。朝、起きて顔を洗い、直ぐにでも歯医者に駆け込みたい気持だった。午前中一番で歯医者に行き、治療をしてもらった。その結果、数段良くなったが、未だ、治療が必要な歯もあるので、来週も来るように言われた。治療済みになるまではしばらくかかるらしい。アルコールは控えるように言われたので、今日は一杯のビールも控えようと思う。通院するだけでも疲れるが、自然と治るはずはないので致し方ない。今日は早く横になって休むつもりだ。

NEW KANJI AND VOCABULARY

NOTES

SET 7

WORDS WITH N3 KANJI (VOLUME 1-2)

様々 (さまざま)	various; varied; diverse; all sorts of	民族上 (みんぞくじょう)	ethnic; racial
王 (おう)	king; ruler; sovereign; monarch	機会 (きかい)	chance; opportunity
もみ消 (け) す	to stub out (e.g. a cigarette); to crush out; to smother (fire); to hush up; to cover up; to stifle; to suppress	結果 (けっか)	result; consequence; outcome; effect
法律上 (ほうりつじょう)	legal; from a legal standpoint; legally speaking; de jure	未成年者 (みせいねんしゃ)	minor; person under age
未満 (みまん)	less than; insufficient	喫煙 (きつえん)	smoking
未成年 (みせいねん)	minor; not of age	文化 (ぶんか)	culture; civilization; civilisation
犯罪 (はんざい)	crime; offence; offense	事件 (じけん)	event; affair; incident; case; plot; trouble; scandal
権利 (けんり)	right; privilege	例 (たと) えば	for example; for instance; e.g.
疑 (うたが) い	doubt; question; uncertainty; skepticism; scepticism; suspicion; distrust	20歳 (はたち)	20 years old
殺 (ころ) し	murder; killing; murderer	盗 (ぬす) み	stealing

ADDITIONAL VOCABULARY

世界 (せかい)	the world; society; the universe	行 (おこな) う	to perform; to do; to conduct oneself; to carry out
歴史 (れきし)	history	重大 (じゅうだい)	serious; important; significant; grave; weighty
固有 (こゆう)	characteristic; traditional; peculiar; inherent; native	罪 (つみ)	crime; sin; wrongdoing; indiscretion
君臨 (くんりん)	reigning; controlling; to reign; to dictate; to control	償 (つぐな) う	to make up for; to compensate for; to indemnify; to recompense; to redeem (e.g. a fault); to atone for
時代 (じだい)	period; epoch; era; age; the times; those days	国 (くに)	country; state; region
歴史書 (れきししょ)	history book	定義 (ていぎ)	definition
書 (か) く	to write; to compose; to pen; to draw; to paint	異 (こと)	difference (from one another); unusual; extraordinary
日本 (にほん)	Japan	違 (ちが) い	difference; distinction; discrepancy; mistake; error
以上 (いじょう)	not less than; ... and more; ... and upwards; beyond ... (e.g. one's means); further (e.g. nothing further to say)	調 (しら) べる	to examine; to look up; to investigate; to check up; to sense; to study; to inquire; to search
大人 (おとな)	adult; grown-up	見 (み) る	to see; to look; to watch; to view; to observe; to examine; to look over; to assess; to check; to judge
意味 (いみ)	meaning; significance; sense	面白 (おもしろ) い	interesting; fascinating; intriguing; enthralling
保護 (ほご)	protection; safeguard; guardianship; custody; patronage	分 (わ) かる	to understand; to comprehend; to grasp; to see; to get; to follow
事実 (じじつ)	fact; truth; reality	飲酒 (いんしゅ)	drinking alcohol (sake)
人 (ひと)	man; person	禁 (きん) じる	to prohibit

SET 7

NEW KANJI AND VOCABULARY

NOTES

SET 7 — VOCABULARY EXERCISE

VOCABULARY				FURIGANA	MEANING	NOTES
事					event; affair; incident; case; plot; trouble; scandal	
文					culture; civilization; civilisation	
					smoking	
	律	上			legal; from a legal standpoint; legally speaking; de jure	
結					result; consequence; outcome; effect	
	会				chance; opportunity	
	え	ば			for example; for instance; e.g.	
					right; privilege	
	い				doubt; question; uncertainty; skepticism; suspicion; distrust	
	し				murder; killing; murderer	
20					20 years old	
	罪				crime; offence; offense	
	年				minor; not of age	
	年	者			minor; person under age	
					less than; insufficient	
も	み		す		to stub out (e.g. a cigarette); to crush out; to smother (fire)	
					king; ruler; sovereign; monarch	
	々				various; varied; diverse; all sorts of	

SET 7

VOCABULARY				FURIGANA	MEANING	NOTES
み					stealing	
族	上				ethnic; racial	

SET 7

世界には様々な歴史があり、また固有の文化がある。王が君臨した時代もあるだろう。歴史書には書かれていない、もみ消されてしまった事件もあったかもしれない。例えば、日本では、法律上、20歳以上が大人とされ、20歳未満は未成年とされている。そのため、20歳未満の犯罪は、権利としてある意味、保護されているのは、疑いのない事実である。しかし、人を殺したり、盗みを行うなどの重大な犯罪はその罪を償わなければならない。国よって、「大人」の定義が異なるのは、民族上の違いがあるからかもしれないが、機会があったら、調べて見ると面白い結果が分かるかもしれない。日本では、未成年者の喫煙や飲酒は禁じられている。それでは、あなたの国はどうですか。

TRANSLATION

SET 7

TRANSLATION

NEW KANJI AND VOCABULARY

NOTES

SET 7

WITH FURIGANA

世界には様々な歴史があり、また固有の文化がある。王が君臨した時代も

あるだろう。歴史書には書かれていない、もみ消されてしまった事件も

あったかもしれない。例えば、日本では、法律上、20歳以上が大人とされ、

20歳未満は未成年とされている。そのため、20歳未満の犯罪は、権利

としてある意味、保護されているのは、疑いのない事実である。しかし、

人を殺したり、盗みを行うなどの重大な犯罪はその罪を償わなければ

ならない。国よって、「大人」の定義が異なるのは、民族上の違いがある

からかもしれないが、機会があったら、調べて見ると面白い結果が分かる

かもしれない。日本では、未成年者の喫煙や飲酒は禁じられている。

それでは、あなたの国はどうですか。

NEW KANJI AND VOCABULARY

NOTES

SET 8 — VOCABULARY

WORDS WITH N3 KANJI (VOLUME 1-2)

学期 (がっき)	school term; semester	熱 (あつ) い	hot (thing); passionate (feelings, etc.); ardent; hot (e.g. gaze)
求 (もと) める	to want; to wish for; to request; to demand; to require; to ask for	港 (みなと)	harbour; harbor; port
由来 (ゆらい)	origin; source; history; derivation	猫 (ねこ)	cat
残 (のこ) る	to remain; to be left	浮 (う) かぶ	to float; to be suspended
演劇部 (えんげきぶ)	drama club (e.g. at school); dramatic society	流 (なが) れ	flow (of a fluid or gas); stream; current; flow (of people, things); passage (of time); tide; passing; (changing) trends; tendency
登山 (とざん)	mountain climbing	花束 (はなたば)	bunch of flowers; bouquet
水泳 (すいえい)	swimming	断 (ことわ) れない	unrefusable; undeclinable
渡航 (とこう)	voyage; passage; travelling	性格 (せいかく)	character (of a person); personality; disposition; nature
留学 (りゅうがく)	studying abroad	単語 (たんご)	word; vocabulary; (usually) single-character word
機会 (きかい)	chance; opportunity	所属 (しょぞく)	belonging to (a group, organization, etc.); affiliation (with); being attached to; being under the control of
深 (ふか) い	deep; profound	得意 (とくい)	triumph; prosperity; pride
溝 (みぞ)	ditch; drain; gutter; trench	短期 (たんき)	short-term
深 (ふか) く	deeply; intimately; heartily; sincerely; profoundly	活発 (かっぱつ)	lively; active; vigorous; animated; brisk
現在 (げんざい)	now; current; present; present time; as of	感 (かん) じる	to feel; to sense; to experience
出産 (しゅっさん)	childbirth; (giving) birth; delivery; parturition; confinement	文化 (ぶんか)	culture; civilization

ADDITIONAL VOCABULARY

私 (わたし)	I; me	結婚 (けっこん)	marriage
娘 (むすめ)	daughter; girl (i.e. a young, unmarried woman)	今度 (こんど)	this time; now
高校生 (こうこうせい)	senior high school student	今 (いま)	now; the present time; just now; soon; immediately
時 (とき)	time; hour; moment	落 (お) ち着 (つ) き	calmness; composure; presence of mind; stability; steadiness
毎 (ごと)	each; every	出 (で) る	to leave; to exit; to go out; to come out; to get out
行 (おこな)	to be done; to be practiced; to be practised; to take place; to be held; to be prevalent; to be in fashion; to be in vogue; to be current; to come into use	船 (ふね)	ship; boat; watercraft; vessel; seaplane

SET 8

ADDITIONAL VOCABULARY

試験 (しけん)	examination; exam; test; trial; experiment	出 (で) ていく	to go out and away; to leave
英語 (えいご)	English (language)	見 (み) える	to be seen; to be in sight; to look; to seem; to appear
教 (おし) える	to teach; to instruct; to tell; to inform; to preach	飼 (か) う	to keep (a pet or other animal); to have; to own; to raise; to rear; to feed
喜 (よろこ) んで	with pleasure	上 (うえ)	above; up; over; elder (e.g. daughter)
学校 (がっこう)	school	まどろむ	to doze (off)
習 (なら) う	to take lessons in; to be taught; to learn (from a teacher); to study (under a teacher); to get training in	行 (い) く	to go; to move (in a direction or towards a specific location); to head (towards); to be transported (towards); to reach
教 (おし) える	to teach; to instruct; to tell; to inform; to preach	雲 (くも)	cloud
話 (はな) す	to talk; to speak; to converse; to chat; to tell; to explain; to narrate	見 (み)	looking; viewing
記憶 (きおく)	memory; recollection; remembrance	遠 (とお) い	far; distant; far away; a long way off; in the distance
高校 (こうこう)	senior high school; high school	国 (くに)	country; state
夏休 (なつやす) み	summer vacation; summer holiday	無事 (ぶじ)	safety; peace; quietness
子 (こ)	child	祈 (いの) る	to pray; to wish
日本 (にほん)	Japan	今月 (こんげつ)	this month
外 (そと)	outside; exterior	誕生月 (たんじょうづき)	month of birth; birthday month
理解 (りかい)	understanding; comprehension; appreciation; sympathy	送 (おく) る	to send (a thing); to dispatch; to despatch; to transmit
人 (じん)	-ian (e.g. Italian); -ite (e.g. Tokyoite); man; person, people [suffix]		

NEW KANJI AND VOCABULARY

NOTES

SET 8

NEW KANJI AND VOCABULARY

NOTES

SET 8

VOCABULARY				FURIGANA	MEANING	NOTES
	い				hot (thing); passionate (feelings, etc.); ardent; hot (e.g. gaze)	
水					swimming	
	来				origin; source; history; derivation	
					ditch; drain; gutter; trench	
	劇	部			drama club (e.g. at school); dramatic society	
	山				mountain climbing	
	る				to remain; to be left	
					harbour; harbor; port	
	学				studying abroad	
	会				chance; opportunity	
出					childbirth; (giving) birth; delivery; confinement	
	航				voyage; passage; travelling	
					cat	
	在				now; current; present; present time; as of	
	く				deeply; intimately; heartily; sincerely; profoundly	
	め	る			to want; to wish for; to request; to demand; to require; to ask for	
	い				deep; profound	
学					school term; semester	

SET 8

VOCABULARY EXERCISE

VOCABULARY				FURIGANA	MEANING	NOTES
発					lively; active; vigorous; animated; brisk	
	じ	る			to feel; to sense; to experience	
	意				triumph; prosperity; pride	
	れ	な	い		unrefusable; undeclinable	
					character (of a person); personality; disposition; nature	
	語				word; vocabulary; (usually) single-character word	
	属				belonging to (a group, org. etc.) affiliation(with); attached to	
短					short-term	
文					culture; civilization	
	れ				flow (of a fluid or gas); stream; current; flow (of people, things)	
花					bunch of flowers; bouquet	
	か	ぶ			to float; to be suspended	

SET 8

私の娘が高校生の時、学期毎に行われる試験の英語を教えたことがある。私は求められると断れない性格なので、喜んで娘が学校で習っている英語を教えたものだ。単語の由来を話した記憶が残っている。娘は高校で演劇部に所属し、登山や水泳も得意で、夏休みにはアメリカに渡航し、短期留学をする活発な子だった。日本の外から、日本をみる機会は、日本とアメリカには深い溝があるのを娘は感じたみたいだが、より深く日本の文化を理解できたと話していた。現在、娘はアメリカ人と結婚し、今度、出産をむかえる。娘は、熱くなりやすい性格だったが、今では落ち着きも出てきたようだ。船が港から出ていくのが見える。飼っている猫は私のひざの上でまどろんでいる。ぽっかり浮かんだ流れ行く雲を見ながら、遠い国の娘の無事を祈るのみだ。今月は娘の誕生月だ。
花束でも送ってみようかな。

TRANSLATION

SET 8

TRANSLATION

NEW KANJI AND VOCABULARY

NOTES

SET 8

WITH FURIGANA

私の娘が高校生の時、学期毎に行われる試験の英語を教えたことがある。

私は求められると断れない性格なので、喜んで娘が学校で習っている英語を

教えたものだ。単語の由来を話した記憶が残っている。娘は高校で演劇部に

所属し、登山や水泳も得意で、夏休みにはアメリカに渡航し、短期留学を

する活発な子だった。日本の外から、日本をみる機会は、日本とアメリカには

深い溝があるのを娘は感じたみたいだが、より深く日本の文化を理解できた

と話していた。現在、娘はアメリカ人と結婚し、今度、出産をむかえる。娘は、

熱くなりやすい性格だったが、今では落ち着きも出てきたようだ。船が港

から出ていくのが見える。飼っている猫は私のひざの上でまどろんでいる。

ぽっかり浮かんだ流れ行く雲を見ながら、遠い国の娘の無事を祈るのみだ。

今月は娘の誕生月だ。花束でも送ってみようかな。

NEW KANJI AND VOCABULARY

NOTES

English Translations

READING COMPREHENSION
SET 1 - 8

READING EXERCISE 1

I'm finally getting married to my beloved boyfriend.

Although It's fun to imagine what kind of ceremony we'll have, it's quite difficult to decide on the location, who to invite, what music to play, who we should ask to give a speech, among other favors, and what to give as a souvenir.

I've been thinking about it since yesterday but I can't decide. Since it's such a sunny day today, let's get ready quickly for a walk and go look at some places and see some people to find ideas before it gets dark.

We'll make it the best!

TRANSLATION

READING EXERCISE 2

To show my gratitude for my wife for all she's done till now, we went on a trip together.

It has been a long time since we traveled, it was over 10 years ago.

After 10 years of working hard and keeping myself busy everyday, I realized that while I have acquired money which I can see and touch, I don't have any special memories with my wife.

As a husband, to even forget your wife's birthday, it's quite shameful.

My wife is naturally calm and gentle, she doesn't get angry, but I feel afraid when I think about whether she's already fed up with me.

I can't change what's already happened in the past but my great hope is that she does not leave me and that we'll always stay together.

I set a reminder on my smart phone for my wife's birthday, just to be sure.

TRANSLATION

READING EXERCISE 3

There are many different types of martial arts, but the one I'm interested in right now is Krav Maga.

Krav Maga, which is also used by the Israeli military, does not rely on an individual's talent. It is easy to learn for a wide variety of people, and is characterized by its combination of striking, foot sweeps and throwing techniques that are designed for real-world combat.

At the very least, as a grown man, I want to be able to protect the people I love, and detest the miserable thought of pitifully being beaten in front of them.

But it's not really to beat and break the bones of the other or any of that sort, the main reason is really that I want to at least be able to remain calm and be accustomed in those kinds of situations.

TRANSLATION

READING EXERCISE 4

Getting into the University of Tokyo is very difficult except for geniuses.

I started attending cram school in order to pass but I am experiencing a great deal of culture shock even though I am a local Japanese. This is because there are a lot of completely different types of people from the kind of environment I've lived in so far. They are people commonly known as 'the elite class'. They have a different perspective and see things on a higher level.

It's only natural for them to spend a lot of money on education and live in prominent, high-end residential areas in Tokyo.

One of the students' parents is a famous politician, and although the image of him is dark and scary on TV, he looked surprisingly normal when he was talking to his son.

Information broadcasted on TV strongly tends to impose an exaggerated image of people after all, so I thought that it's important to actually see it yourself.

TRANSLATION

READING EXERCISE 5

I played baseball from elementary to junior high school. I looked awkward when I was starting out but I practiced everyday. I actively participated in games that we could sign up for and gained experience.

When I was in junior high, after school, I was a member of a club doing extracurricular activities and played actively as leadoff hitter and third baseman.
Although we advanced to the finals in our last tournament in junior high school, the opposing team scored four points and we eventually lost 4-1, but in my head it remains as a good memory.
In those days, I had fast legs and could steal when I got on base. If I speak of what I really wanted, I would have liked to have won the championship and qualified for the next higher level tournament, but we all worked together as a team and did our best, and even though it felt frustrating to lose at the time, I'm more than content now.

TRANSLATION

READING EXERCISE 6

When I ate something hard yesterday, I felt something wrong with my teeth. To my surprise, a part of my tooth was chipped out. I felt I was getting old, but it gradually became painful and I couldn't sleep well that night because it hurt.

It felt like wanting to wake up the next morning, wash my face and rush to the dentist right away. I went to the dentist first in the morning and had myself treated. As a result, I got a lot better but I still had some teeth that needed treatment, so I was told to come back next week.

It seems the treatment will take some time to complete. I was told to refrain from alcohol, so I think I'll restrain myself from having a glass of beer today.

I get tired just going for treatment regularly but since I don't expect it to get better on its own, I don't have a choice. I'm going to lie down and rest early today.

TRANSLATION

READING EXERCISE 7

There are varied histories in the world as well as unique cultures. There may have been times when kings reigned. There may have been incidents covered up that were not written in history books. For example, in Japan, by law, those over 20 years of age are considered adults and those under 20 are considered minors. Therefore, it is an undeniable fact that those under the age of 20 who commit a crime are protected, in a sense, as a right. However, serious offences such as killing or stealing are crimes that must be paid for. The definition of "adult" may vary from country to country because of ethnic differences, but if you have a chance, you may find out some interesting results if you look into it. In Japan, it is prohibited for minors to smoke and drink. What about your country?

TRANSLATION

READING EXERCISE 8

When my daughter was in high school, I taught her English for exams held every semester. I'm not one to say no when asked, so I gladly taught her the English she was learning at school. I still remember discussing the origin of words. She was a very active girl who was a member of the drama club in high school, was good at mountain climbing and swimming, and traveled to the United States during summer vacation to study abroad for a short period of time.

She said that the opportunity to see Japan from the outside helped her understand Japanese culture more deeply, although she felt that there seemed like a deep gap between Japan and America.

She is now married to an American and is expecting a baby. She used to be hot-tempered, but now she seems to have calmed down.

I can see the ship leaving the harbor. My cat is slumbering in my lap.

I can only pray for my daughter's safety in a faraway land while watching the clouds drift by.

It's my daughter's birthday this month. Maybe I should send her a bouquet of flowers.

TRANSLATION

CHECK OUT OUR OTHER BOOKS

Kanji Essentials Practice Workbook: JLPT N3 Intermediate I - Volume 1

Book Sales Page

To get your copy, scan this QR code to take directly to the book's sales page on Amazon.

Kanji Essentials Practice Workbook: JLPT N3 Intermediate I - Volume 3

Book Sales Page

To get your copy, scan this QR code to take directly to the book's sales page on Amazon.

Kanji Essentials Practice Workbook: JLPT N4 - Kanji Beginner Series

Book Sales Page

To get your copy, scan this QR code to take directly to the book's sales page on Amazon.

CHECK OUT OUR OTHER BOOKS

Kanji Essentials Practice Workbook: JLPT N5
Kanji Beginner Series

To get your copy, scan this QR code to take directly to the book's sales page on Amazon.

Book Sales Page

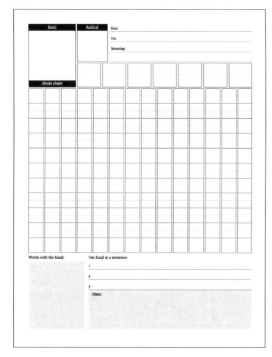

NEED MORE PRACTICE SHEETS?

Check out the Author's page to get a selection of Kanji writing practice notebooks.

For more details, scan the QR code below to take you directly to the author's page on Amazon:

Author's Page

Kanji Essentials Practice Notebooks

Choose from classic cover designs. More options can be found on the author's page on Amazon. Scan the QR code to view selections.

Did this book help you in any way on your language learning journey?

LEAVE A REVIEW

A biggest thank you for purchasing and using this book. We are honored to be part of your Japanese language learning journey and truly hope that you've gotten the most out of our workbook series.

If you enjoyed this book and have a few minutes to spare, please consider leaving a review on Amazon.

Getting feedback from reviews on Amazon really do make a difference. We make sure to read all reviews and would love to hear your thoughts.

Kanji Essentials Practice Workbook: JLPT N3 VOLUME 2 Book Review Page

(You might be asked to log in to your Amazon account to allow you to do so.)

Getting feedback from reviews on Amazon really do make a difference. We make sure to read all reviews and would love to hear your thoughts.

COMMENTS AND SUGGESTIONS

If you have any comments or suggestions to make this book better or if you spot any errors which you want the author to correct, please email kanjiessentials.workbook@gmail.com.

漢字
KANJI
E S S E N T I A L S

Made in the USA
Middletown, DE
14 June 2021